AUTISM: In My Own Words

AUTISM: In My Own Words

Jaylon V. O'Neal

authorHOUSE®

AuthorHouse™
1663 Liberty Drive
Bloomington, IN 47403
www.authorhouse.com
Phone: 1-800-839-8640

Published by AuthorHouse   01/22/2013

ISBN: 978-1-4817-0920-0 (sc)
ISBN: 978-1-4817-0918-7 (hc)
ISBN: 978-1-4817-0919-4 (e)

Library of Congress Control Number: 2013901155

To my mother, who is my rock, sword and shield and to all the people who ran, backed out and thought that I would never amount to anything

Chapter 1

My mom would always tell me:

"Son, I would never tell you anything wrong."

And she was right because on September 30, 2011, my sweet 16th birthday, the truth was finally revealed to me. I received the best birthday gift ever. She sat me down like she often did and said with concern in her **tone**:

"You are autistic."

It was like a mountain of burden had been lifted off of me. I was finally free. Free of all the uncertainty, doubt and shame that came with the sixteen years of bondage. I knew what autism was because I had researched it years ago. My mom turned me on to the movie *Rain Man* and it became one of my favorite movies. (Go Figure). The character Raymond Babbitt played by Dustin Hoffman captivated me and I wanted to know more. I tend to thoroughly research things that I'm interested in and Raymond's photographic memory resonated with me. I could look at a periodic table once and chart it exactly. I could recite a sonnet without preparation. Raymond repeats himself as a tape recorder would, but I repeat my sentences because I believe they sound better the 2nd time. I sometimes wish I could be Raymond Babbitt because he had no sense of love or emotion and in this world; you need a suit of armor to protect you from the land of the ignorant and home of the fearful.

September 30, 1995. That was the day I was born. Before that moment, no one knew me, my capabilities or what I was destined to be. That day went down in history as the greatest day of my mom's life. After 15 hours of labor, she delivered a healthy baby boy. She named me Jaylon after the famous (now retired) basketball player Jalen Rose and from that day forward, I was known by the name of Jaylon Vishawn O'Neal, but that wouldn't be the only name that I would be called.

At a very early age, my mom told me that I didn't process information the same as everyone else and that it was their problem if they didn't understand me. She noticed very early that I wasn't like other kids so she took me to several doctors in hopes that they could find the answer. It turns out that in their mind, I was a lost cause. No one could figure me out. She also had doctors tell her that "I was never going to be an intelligent person" or "I was never going to be like everyone else." It hurt my mom to realize that these doctors that she believed was going to help had little faith in me. That's when she made her move.

My mom got a piece of brown cardboard and drew and colored all the things that I should know. She drew a house and labeled "House" under it. She drew a tree and labeled "Tree" under it.

She colored all of the colors on the board and labeled under them the corresponding name for that particular color. She wrote all the letters of the alphabet and numbers one thru fifty and their names on the board.

We worked on that board every day for hours. She was convinced that I would succeed no matter what.

At age 3, my mother, grandma and I moved from Chicago to Georgia. I've lived in Georgia for 13 years now and I've spent all of those years trying to find out the answer to my universal questions:

- Why don't people want to be around me?
- Why do people treat me differently?
- Why am I the "odd person out?"
- Why can't people understand who I am?

It's because of questions like these that made me become a loner. I didn't have many friends; I've never had a girlfriend or even graced the list of a party invite. Life for me was very lonely. I felt insecure and became very antisocial. It was easier that way. I was the type of person that you would just say "Hi", "Goodbye", or have to get serious with. The thing about me is I would always perceive things differently, so I won't always see eye-to-eye with people at times. For example, when people tell me a joke, it would take me a minute to actually realize what that joke meant. Also, when people are trying to tell me things, they need to be direct and not beat-around-the-bush with the information because otherwise, I may get thrown off and not get what they're saying.

Another thing is people may not want to be around me because of the way that I act and how silly I get at times. I mean, I know when to calm down and be mature around others, but I end up taking it to the extreme when I have fun. I like to be around people that actually **want** to be around me and for years that has been a fine few. After seventeen years of living on this Earth, I have realized that the only life that I can control is my own, but to judge me without knowing me is a disservice to me. I can't make anyone understand my struggle but I know that having this disorder has strengthened my character and made me a better person.

Ok, here are a few things about me that you should know. I love playing video games with a passion! One of my favorite games is *Call of Duty*. I play *Call of Duty* with my friends online on my *PS3* and we have fun every time. I like to dance, rap, draw, write, speak publicly and I hope to become an actor/rapper one day. My favorite food is chicken, my favorite beverage is Sprite and my favorite dessert is chocolate cake. I like to listen to Old School Music because rap today isn't what it's used to be. One of my favorite television shows is *Married with Children*. I watch that show every morning before I go to school. I love that show so much because it's funny and the scenarios that the family get into in every episode are hilarious!

One of my favorite movies is *The Back to the Future Trilogy*. In my opinion, the Back to the Future movies is hands down, the best sci-fi movies ever created. I can watch all 3 of the Back to the Future movies over and over again and never get bored. I also say that Michael J. Fox is one of the best actors that I've ever seen.

Also, I am a huge Michael Jackson fan. I listen to all of his songs, watch all of his videos, performed all of his dance moves, etc. The 1st song that got me hooked to him was *Beat It*. When I first heard it, I played it over and over again until I got the entire song stuck in my head. From then on, I was just trying to be "Like Mike". It made me real depressed when he died. That tore up my whole world. I felt like I died with him. I realized what the phrase "You don't know what you have until it's gone" meant because never in a million years would I have ever imagined that he would be gone. That made me realize that life is precious and shouldn't be wasted. He made his mark in history and this is where I make mine. It all started when I was four years old.

Growing up in Georgia, I really didn't know what to expect from a place that I had never been to. We moved to an apartment complex and I loved it. We had a pool and a basketball court. I was in heaven!

One thing that I enjoyed doing out of all the things in the world was play my Nintendo 64. I liked to play Super Smash Bros Brawl Melee on my Nintendo 64. If not that, then I would play NBA Jam until my game started breaking. The one thing that I thought was amazing from that game was when a basketball player that looked like Yao Ming did a front flip dunk into the basket. After that, I shut off the game because that blew my mind.

There was one night that I remember that changed my life. I don't remember what I was doing at the time, but I do remember that my grandma wanted me to sit with her at the family table. She had the book *Cat in the Hat* in her hand and we start reading. What she was doing was she wasn't reading to me, she was teaching me ***how*** to read.

It was one of the moments that you would have with your family that you look back on when you're older and say "Thank you for caring." It was a milestone to know how to read and it was a precious milestone that I'll always hold near and dear to my heart to have spent quality time with my beloved grandmother.

Entering Head Start was a huge step because the doctors told my mom that I would never be in mainstream education. At the time, I was real nervous because I wasn't use to being around anyone except my family. When I got there, I was met by little kids. They were playing with toys, reading books, running around with other kids, etc. You know usual stuff. My mom went to go talk to the two women in charge of the school to tell them about me. She said her usual "Goodbye! I love you!" to me and left. Then it was just me by myself.

I served as the outsider in Head Start because I didn't want to be around other people that much. My mom told me that at that age I always wanted to be by myself. She said that I hated being away from her I didn't like things that weren't familiar so I would cry when she left me and some days until she came back to get me. I loved and had to have structure early on and still today I hate change of any sort. My mom had a routine that we followed. She would wake me up, make me brush my teeth, wash my face and dress myself. I only ate maple brown sugar oatmeal for breakfast nothing else I didn't like anything else. Oh and I had to tie my own shoes. She said it took me so long to learn how to tie my shoes that once I learned that she would never tie them again. My mother had to teach me everything. She was teaching me things to make me independent.

Her expectations for me were very clear:

- Go to school
- Make it through the day without crying
- Learn my lessons
- Leave
- Repeat.
  That's it.

Being that autism wasn't talked about much in the early 90's, we didn't know much about it so we had to figure it out ourselves. So every time something odd happened with me, my mom would record it in her journal. For example, one day, my mom picked me up from Head Start and drove me home. The radio was on and she turned the volume all the way up. Then, the CD began to skip and I went crazy. She said I started hitting my chair and screaming so she quickly turned the radio off. That scared the mess out of my mom and for the rest of the ride home, it was silent. We later found out that I was sensitive to noise and that I have sensory processing difficulties. The loud music would make my ears ring. That's why every time you see me in public; I have ear plugs in my ears. I hate loud sounds like a bus screeching its brakes or nails on a chalkboard! It irritates the heck out of me and as soon as I hear it . . . *I GO OFF!* When my mom explained why my ears were so sensitive, I felt as if I was given a superhuman ability and the screaming and the hitting was my way of dealing with it.

When I got home, the 1st thing that I did was say "Hello" to my grandmother who was sitting on the couch watching television. After that, I went to my room and played my Nintendo 64. I started to play Mario Kart until I got tired. The thing that I like about my Nintendo 64 was that I had a lot of games for it, so I was entertained for days and days. My mom told me that I had a long history when it came to Nintendo 64s because it seems that every time I got one, I would always break it doing something stupid like dropping it on the floor or yanking the plugs out of the wall. She always talked about how spoiled I was and how my family loved spoiling me because I was the baby. Now that I look back at that moment of my life, I was the only male child. My grandmother was thrilled to finally have a little boy running around. She only had 2 children; my mom and my aunt Marsha, so a boy was Christmas all over again which was just what she needed.

When I wasn't playing on my Nintendo 64, I would be watching television. I had a lot of favorite television shows on TV. There was *Rocko's Modern Life, Angry Beavers, Cat Dog, Doug, AAAHHH!!! Monsters!, Cow and Chicken, Dexter's Laboratory, Scooby Doo, Looney Tunes!* I loved them all! But none of them ever came close to my favorite TV show: *Tom and Jerry.* There was nothing like Tom and Jerry! A blue cat that's always being outsmarted by a clever mouse. You just can't make good TV like Tom and Jerry. I would always laugh for hours because the show was just that funny! I've seen every episode of that show and there's never a time that I would get bored from watching Tom and Jerry! Ever! I even played the video game that was based on the show! I was a huge fan of Tom and Jerry at the time and still am to this day!

Later that day, I went to bed. I slept in my toddler bed in my mom's room. The one thing that I remember about bedtime is my grandmother was always writing in her diary. She wrote about her faith, her battle with cancer and her love for her family. It was her way of expressing her innermost thoughts and feelings. As I look back, I'm glad that she had it, so my family can have something to hold onto. In it contained words and loving memories from our beloved mother and grandmother in her own words. That's better than silver and gold! Back then, I didn't see the importance of that diary because I was too young to understand what it meant, but now I realize that's more than just a book, it's a keepsake that will last forever.

Enjoy the life that you live and enjoy being a kid regardless of how different you are.

Chapter 2

—◦✦◦—

In the year 2000, a lot of things happened.

One

Everyone in the United States felt **real** stupid when Y2K didn't happen.

Two

My mom got married on October 27, 2000.

Three

My little sister, Jasmine, was born on May 30, 2000.

Four

I turned 5 years old.

Five

I started kindergarten at Ocean Way Elementary School.

On the day before I started school at Ocean Way, I watched a *Buzz Lightyear* cartoon movie and for some reason, it would benefit my character the following day.

On the 1st day of school, my teacher was Ms. Jane Wilder. She was as sweet as an apple picked fresh off the tree. A couple of minutes after everyone came into the classroom; she wanted everyone to sit on her colorful carpet. Since I was the type of person to draw attention to myself, I jumped on the carpet while saying "To Infinity and Beyond!" That's when all the kids in the classroom started to laugh and Ms. Wilder told everyone to be quiet. Ms. Wilder had another teacher in her classroom just like in Head Start. I don't remember her name, but I know that she always had Ms. Wilder's back.

The one thing that I remember is that I was placed in the special class for some reason. I was always pulled out of my regular class to talk to a woman named Mrs. Evans and then sent back to my regular class. I didn't understand why, but it really wasn't a problem for me. I mean, I wasn't mad or anything. I was just neutral about the entire thing. I would go there for a couple of minutes and then go back to my regular class in Ms. Wilder's room as usual.

I was still in a classroom with regular kids, but it happened to me and only me. I wasn't sure why this was happening, but like I said before, I had neutral feelings over the subject. I did meet some people who were also in the special class just like I was. There was a boy named David who talked funny. I don't know if it was a speech impediment or what, but I didn't really care. I also meet a boy named Jonathan. He was a nice boy that really didn't look like anything was wrong with him. Kind of like me, but for some reason whenever we would have lunch, the cafeteria staff would give him peanut butter and jelly sandwiches every day. Then I met Shane. A dude that was nice to hang with, but had a halitosis problem every time he spoke. Also, whenever he talked, it was difficult to understand. All and all they were good people that I would hang out with when I was in the special class.

When I was in Ms. Wilder's class, I may have been different from everyone else in the classroom, but I was a kid just like everyone else. I did things like everyone, learned like everyone else, and acted like everyone else, so I thought I was that type of different that was unexplainable. Almost as if I was an alien of some sort that was stranded on a desolate wasteland that had an advantage over the remaining population of people that lived on the planet. If only I knew what that advantage was.

One of the things that I remember from Ms. Wilder's class is that she never ended a day of school without telling us this story. You see, the story was an adventure that wasn't in a book, but on a chart. It was about these kids going into the forest or something like that and they were trying to find treasures in the forest. The part that I remember from that book was when one of them falls into a hole or finds a hole. I would always want to know what happened or who went missing in the forest. I mean, the story was entertaining to me and I would hate it when it would be time to go because then we wouldn't know the epic conclusion to the story. To this day, I still don't know what happened, but it's amazing that I can remember that story and where we left off in the story.

One of the most infamous moments of my life was when I went to the doctor and how that visit paralyzed me for the rest of my life. My mom and dad took me to the doctor's office for my annual checkup as usual. We sat in the waiting room and waited for the doctor to call either my name or my mother's name. A couple of minutes later, one of the doctors called us in. We walked in the room and they checked my ears, heartbeat, breathing, pulses, weight, height, temperature, the whole 9 yards. But after that, it all went downhill when the doctor did this one procedure.

He took out a tongue depressor and tried to get it into my mouth. I wouldn't open my mouth which slightly agitated him. Everyone tried to get me to stick my tongue out, but I just wouldn't let that stick anywhere near my mouth. That's when everyone held me down on the operating bed. That's when they were in complete control. My mouth was open, he put the tongue depressor in my mouth and that's when it happened. *I threw up everywhere!*

I was in so much pain and that's when things started to get serious. I was so upset at that man for what he did to get me to vomit all over the floor! He left the room and I sat on a chair trying to relieve myself of the pain I was experiencing. The doctor would walk back and forward outside the door saying "Jaylon" over and over again in a monotone voice. I just watched him while my head just swung from side to side and my mouth stayed open. I felt helpless and victimized. I felt like I was in a Doctor Kevorkian scenario or something. We left the hospital with my parents saying that I had a clean bill of health. My parents went to *Blockbuster* to rent a movie and I told my mom:

"Mommy, I don't want to go to the doctor anymore."

My mom looked back at me and said:

"I know baby. I know."

Since then, I always had a fear of tongue depressors. I just hope that after that incident, I hope that I never have anything like that ever again in my life.

2001

A lot of things happened in the year 2001.
One
My Grandma Michelle lost her battle with cancer and passed away
Two
My family and I moved to Fort Benning
Three
9/11
Four
I turn 6 and I started 1st grade

When Grandma Michelle died, my mom was absolutely broken. She lost her mother, the most important person in her entire life. She was the person that gave birth to her and the one person that help make her the mother she is today. Without her, I really wouldn't appreciate reading or the power that it has. It also meant that when she died, I lost one of the most prominent fighters of my life because whenever I was being badmouthed by someone, she would fight back against that person. She believed just like my mother that I should have a fighting chance in this life and that no one should take me down. She was my sword, my shield and my fighter. I love her and I miss her.

Grandma Michelle

1956-2001

<u>R.I.P.</u>

When we lived in Fort Benning, I found nothing wrong with it. I mean, I moved before so it was nothing different. The one thing that I enjoyed was the fact that so many kids lived around me, meaning that I would make a lot of friends. I met a boy named Jacob who lived across the street from me. He was a boy that I often played with but he made me so mad one day. He threw a football straight at my stomach on purpose. And that ended our friendship. I went to school the next day and I met these two brothers. They were both cool to me. I enjoyed hanging out with both of them. We did everything together. Then I met another boy named Tray. Tray had to be one of the best friends that I could make because he was so awesome. He loved DragonBall Z, video games, and doing back flips on my trampoline. He was a good friend to have.

When I went to school, I would walk to school. To be honest, there really wasn't a reason to be driven to the school or take a bus to the school because we lived ***right*** by the school. I was always walking either by myself or with Tray. We would always talk about whatever was on our minds. It didn't matter what it was. I just wanted someone to listen. I found out that he was older than me by a year; he was a grade higher than I was, and he was incredibly smart. He was always telling me an interesting fact that I never thought I'd need to know in the future like how black widow spiders eat their male or how whales weigh.

When I got into the building, he went to his teacher and I went to mine. My teacher's name was Ms. Dove. Ms. Dove was as sweet as cherry pie. I mean, she loved us as if we were her children. She was always sweet and I never remember seeing her get mad at anyone in the class.

She was so sweet that some boys that were friends of mine sung a song about her called D-O-V-E. The only problem that she had was she loved to eat fish. She would always be talking to people with her fishy breath. It wasn't until I told her that she had bad breath that she started to do something about it. One day after lunch, she came to me and asked me:

"Jaylon, what do you smell?"

She blew her breath in my face and it smelled like toothpaste. I told her:

"Tooth."

I said "Tooth" because I was caught off-guard by the question and didn't know how to respond to the question. That was the only problem that I had with Ms. Dove. After that, everything was good but I would always just say what was on my mind whether it was good or bad. I said it and she started to look at me in an entirely different way. When that problem was resolved, I was in the beginning of my own problems. First off, I accidentally said something about a woman named Mrs. Cleaver and her marriage and everything went hazy for a moment. All I asked was:

"Are you married?"

I guess she got offended by it. I mean, I didn't want it to go down that road, but it did.

Another thing that I did wrong was something that I would go back in time and slap myself for. It was violent, barbaric, and it was by far one of the worst things that I could ever do to another human being. I don't know how it all happened, but I actually **choked** another student with my bare hands. I never thought that I would be doing something like that in my life, but I did. I apologized a million times to him and he forgave me, but 2 wrongs don't make a right. This last thing that I did was truly unacceptable and pretty much is the reason why I don't fight other people.

In Ms. Dove's class, she wanted us to do a play called *Three Billy Goats Gruff.* We were all assigned our role in the play and me along with my friend Damon Jones were the sound effects. Another student came towards the microphone that I was supposed to speak into and started playing around with it. That's when I did the dumbest thing I could think of. I punched him in the face. I mean, that's what I felt I needed to do. It wasn't the answer, but I let my feelings get the best of me. After that, I got detention for the 1st time in my life and I didn't participate in the play. My mom got the report of what happened and she gave me the punishment of a lifetime. I wasn't allowed to do anything! I wasn't allowed to touch the TV set, go outside, play my video games, play with my friends, nothing. I guess this is what happens when you let your let your feelings get the best of you. Think before you act.

A year passed and second grade at Bayside Elementary School started off good. My new teacher's name was Mrs. Andrews and she was as nice as Ms. Dove. One of the things that I remember about Mrs. Andrews was that she had a son named Tony that had a class next door from Mrs. Andrews. Another thing that I remember is that she would always kiss you on the cheek if you did something right in her class. Another thing she would do is she would never end the school day without reading a Junie B. Jones book to the class and singing "Zippity Doo-Da."

One of the things that I remember changed how I approach other people socially. It also showed me what it means to have a friend or lose a friend based on how you act around that friend and how you make that friend feel. It was the day where I met a boy named Joseph.

He was the new kid at the school and I thought he was pretty awesome. He was black just like me and he liked to have fun just like me. I introduced myself to him and he introduced himself to me. We introduced ourselves to each other and we pretty much did everything together. We'd play on the playground, jump on my trampoline, and play with other kids. I mean, we were inseparable. Then one day, he came to me with his bike. His bike had two wheels on it and he asked me if I wanted to ride bikes with him.

I told him that I couldn't because I didn't know how to ride a 2-wheeled bike. I told my parents about the problem of not being able to ride a 2-wheeled bike and that's when they sprang into action. They went out, bought a bike for me and my dad showed me how to ride a bike for the 1st time. I got on the bike, he held me down to the seat, I pedaled forward a little bit to get some speed in and soon enough, he let go. That's when I started pedaling all by myself down the street! I couldn't believe it! Now, I knew how to ride a two-wheeled bike and now I could ride with my friends wherever they wanted to ride to!

Since I knew how to ride a bike, my friends and I rode everywhere. We rode around my neighborhood, around the block, past my school, and we even rode to his house. We even raced each other! It seems that every time I see Joseph, we would always end up riding all over the place and we would always be having fun in the process. That's why I believed it was going to be a beautiful friendship.

Then, there was this one day in school where Joseph came to school with a large afro. Everyone was surprised to see that afro because a couple of days ago, his hair was braided and all of a sudden, his hair exploded! I mean, I didn't care if he had an afro; I was just surprised that it came at such a quick pace. I didn't know the natural hair process

16

because my hair was always cut short and neatly edged. We were still good friends and everything, but something told me that I was doing something wrong at some point. For some reason when I wanted to hang with him after school, he didn't for some strange reason.

One day I went to go find him and see if he was outside. I saw him relaxing in the street with one of his friends and I went to where he was and said:

"Hey, Joseph!"

He looked at me and said:

"Who's Joseph? I'm not Joseph!"

Then he started covering his face, so I wouldn't see him. I mean, it's like he didn't want to be around me. Like I wasn't his friend anymore and I didn't do anything wrong to him!

I said:

"Come on, Joseph. Don't be like that! I wanted to tell you about this movie that I saw!"

He said again:

"I told you dude. I don't know who you are!"

I said:

"What's wrong man? Are you OK?"

He said:

"Alright! Fine! I'm Joseph! OK! I'm Joseph! And you don't even have to tell me the movie you seen! It was SpongeBob SquarePants!"

I looked at him with a confused look and laughed. I said:

"No man! I seen the movie *Scooby Doo 2: Monsters Unleashed.*"

That's when I got on my bike and left the block because I believed that he didn't want to be around me anymore. But the truth was his parents were divorcing and Joseph was moving away. His sadness had nothing to do with me. He was just going through a terrible time and I wasn't aware of it. After that, I never saw Ryan again. I didn't know where he was going and I didn't know why he never told me he was leaving, but I knew I lost a great friend in the process. I guess that's life, isn't it? You meet new people, you share new experiences with them and move on. And speaking of moving on, I had a little bit of moving to do myself.

Think before you act and appreciate the friends and family that you have because you never know when they will leave your life forever.

Chapter 3

———————— ❁ ————————

One thing happened in the year 2002 that made all the difference in my family. We added a new addition to the family. My little brother, Keith, was born on July 11, 2002.

Towards the end of second grade, my family finally got enough money to buy their very own house and that meant we were moving away. When we went to the house to check it out, I saw that it was one of the largest houses in the entire neighborhood. It had a front yard, a back yard and a side yard. We went inside the house and checked it out. The house had 3 bedrooms, 3 bathrooms, a living room, a downstairs den, a basement, a kitchen, a back yard patio, a shed and a fireplace. My parents had the bedroom with the bathroom in it (of course), my little sister had her own bedroom and me and my little brother had to share. We both had to sleep in bunk beds and I had the top bunk. (Fortunately for me, that didn't last long because I later moved into the basement downstairs!)

As for the situation at school, my mom had to drive me from the new house all the way to Fort Benning in order for me to go to school. I told Mrs. Andrews all about the new house and she asked me:

"What was wrong with your old house?"

I told her:

"It had too many cracks in the wall and it was caving in."

She said:

"Oh. Do you like your new house?"

I said:

"Yeah! It's awesome!"

It was conversations like that that made me miss Mrs. Andrews. I miss everything about that teacher. Her smile, her wits, and her kisses. But it was time for me to move on. It was time for me to set out for new life and that's just what I did.

When I went to 3rd grade, I went back to Ocean View Elementary. Only things started to play out a bit differently than I expected. Going back to Ocean View pretty much meant the same routine from kindergarten all over again which meant that I was placed back in the special class. Well . . . , I guess that's one of the things that I had to look forward to this year. I mean, the thing about the special class was it's not that I didn't like it, it's just that every time I go in there, I always look at myself and ask "Am I slow or something?" I mean, the whole thing just made me wonder "What is wrong with me?" I often also wondered "Why was my mom always at the school?" Am I that bad? I found out later that she had to attend an IEP meeting with all my teachers to put together a plan to meet all my "autistic" needs. She also would just randomly pop up to see how I was doing. I just thought she was the parent of the month *every month.*

I went inside my 3rd grade class and, for some reason, it reminded me of Mrs. Andrews. Mainly because in my opinion, my teacher, Mrs. Gibbens, looked *exactly* like Mrs. Andrews. Also, she had a son named Joe that was *in the classroom directly next to mine.* What a coincidence! It was as if Mrs. Andrews followed me all the way back to Ocean View Elementary and brought her son with her. I mean, dang!

She didn't give kisses, but everything else was pretty much the same.

I also remember my 1st crush. Her name was Ashley Dennis. She was a very attractive girl that I liked very much. I used to feel that way around a girl named Brittany Cecil, but I moved. I mean, at that time, I was all over Ashley. I started talking to her, being around her, hanging out with her, everything. Then I did something wrong. After lunch one day, I made my move too early! She went to class and I followed her. I brought my heart up to tell her how I really feel about her.

I said:

"Ashley. There's something I want to tell you."

She said:

"What?"

I said:

"I h-have a-a-a-a crush on you!"

That's when everything went down south. And that's when she said:

"Oh. Jaylon, I only like you as a friend."

When I heard that, my heart just wasn't the same. I mean, that's why I shouldn't have high expectations because the higher they are, the harder it's going to hurt when you get rejected. At that moment, all I felt inside was hurt because I liked this girl as much as I like chicken. That's when I sat down in my seat and chilled for a bit. Ashley and I still remain friends to this day and I will always remember that day.

I could always meet new people, but keeping their friendship was another thing. I remember meeting Tommy Bevin. When I met Tommy, we became best friends at the blink of an eye because we had a lot of things in common. For example, we both enjoy watching World Wrestling Entertainment and we both like the wrestler John Cena. We would talk for hours on end about John Cena and we would also sing songs from his album that we listened to. We were the best of friends at the time. It's like everything that had to do with World Wrestling Entertainment; we would talk about over and over. If a pay-per-view event came on demand, he would always be the one who seen it and he would tell me everything that happened. One time, he told me that if he had money, he would buy the John Cena chain that he wears around his neck or he would buy the clean version of his album that he released in '05. I told him that if I ever got money, I would buy it for him, but I never did. I mean, hey! It was the thought that counts! Am I right?

The one thing that I remember that made me feel bad was when I heard that he was moving to Alabama when school was over. That meant that I was never going to see him again, so I decided to spend as much time with him around school as possible. When he came into the school, all we did was talking about wrestling, John Cena, and whatever was on our mind. We were just trying to make the moments that we had wonderful memories because the end of the school year was right around the corner. The one thing that I miss about Tommy is that he treated me as an equal. He didn't treat me like I was a "special" person or a straight-up idiot. That's the one thing that I miss about Tommy Bevin.

As we walked down the hallway to reach the exit, we both sung the lyrics to "I'm A Bad Man" by John Cena. It wasn't until we finally reach the exit of the school building and said good-bye that I realized that I lost a great friend. I felt like I was never going to find a good friend like him because he was like my friends Tyler and Joseph in Fort Benning. I mean, he made me feel like I was an actual person which is what people should start doing. At that point in time, I wished that more people would be just like him.

As I entered the 4th grade at Ocean View, my year at the school started to take a turn for the worst and I didn't even know how. But I do know that it had something to do with how different I was from everyone else in the world. It all started when I met my new teacher Mrs. Simmons.

Mrs. Simmons was a middle age woman that was very wise. She was always being nice to everyone and she also made it fun to be in her classroom. I mean, she loved having me in her class because she knew how smart I was. I mean, I may say things differently, I may need a minute to process information at times and I may also blurt out things and say the answer when it was already said, but none of that makes me a stupid person. And it was because of those traits that made me a target for people.

For example, one of the things that I remember distinctly was when I meet River Bidden. Now, when I met River, we were cool. I mean, that's how it started out. Then, that's where things started to go down. River and I would constantly be going back and forth at each other until we just stopped being friends.

After that, he started making fun of the fact that I was in the special class. He once called me a "buck-toothed Special Ed head". Then I started to feel ashamed of myself over something that I had no control over. Because back then, every negative thing that was directed towards me, I took it as the hardest thing on Earth. I mean, I was that sensitive towards everything negative and I was always questioning myself on why I had to have this life.

- Why am I getting picked on?
- Why am I in the special class?
- Why can't anyone accept me for who I am?

To me, it's like I had a disease that prevented everyone else from being around me. A lifelong disease that stayed with me forever because I could only be friends with a few people. A lot of people *knew me,* but they weren't friends with me. I don't know why life for me was like that, but it was something that I just had to deal with.

Another thing that I remember from 4th grade was when I had a crush on another girl named Kathy Fowler. Kathy was the type of girl that talked in an accent that makes you think of rodeos, horseback riding, and country music, but she was gorgeous all the same. I mean, she loved horses and country music **with a passion!** It's like every time she spoke, it would always be about horses. She would always talk about riding a horse, rubbing the horse's mane, and feeling the wind blow through her hair as she rode the horse down the field.

That's when I wanted to get to know Kathy, but then that's when I did something wrong. I made my move too fast again! I went to her and told her that I had a crush on her and she told me the same thing that Ashley told me.

"I like you as a friend!"

I may have been hurt by that same comment over and over again, but that never stopped me from going after Kathy. It was just something about her that made me feel like an emotional magnet towards her. I mean, she was beautiful to me and I didn't want to stop loving her.

I didn't want to offend her either. I still have that problem now. I just had to figure out a way to get out of the friend zone, but it wouldn't come to me in 4th grade.

I remember that I was known for being smart and for being the class clown. I was the person that would always try to speak for the entire class, making everyone in the class laugh or become the center of attention whether I wanted to be or not. If anything, that is the one thing that I was remembered for in the 4th grade. In subjects that interest me, I was always one step ahead of everyone, but in areas that bored me, it took me a minute to wrap my brain around certain things. I just excelled in things that excited me and did OK in other areas. What's "special" about that? It's because of these qualities that I have that made me different from contemporary society, but I don't care if I'm different. In fact, why should I? The world would be boring if everyone was the same and this is just me being me.

In fifth grade, my vision of how I saw reality changed dramatically. It wasn't until that I met a man that showed me through humor and hardcore discipline that play time was over. He also showed me that it's okay to be yourself even if nobody likes it. It wasn't until I met my 5th grade teacher, Mr. Dan, that I understood what I was really in school for. He knew that we were kids and that kids loved to play around and have fun, but he wanted us to realize that school was a place of business even if he had to yell at us a million times just for us to grasp the concept.

Looking back, I characterized Mr. Dan as the "Al Bundy" of the 5th grade because of his sense of humor and his recaps of the mid or late 20th century. He would always have everyone in the classroom laughing because he would have a joke up his sleeve. It wasn't until that one dreadful day that the students in Mr. Dan's class realized that what happened next wouldn't be a laughing matter.

One day, we were going over our spelling words in his class when a girl named Katherine Pitts, who I've known since kindergarten, was spelling the word cucumber. She spelled C-U-C-U— . . . when out of the blue, Mr. Dan said in sudden pain:

"Get the phone! Call the office!"

I couldn't believe my eyes! Mr. Dan was having a heart attack in the classroom! Students opened the classroom door and yelled out into the halls:

"HELP! SOMEONE HELP!"

That's when a teacher came and got everyone out of Mr. Dan's classroom and into her classroom until help arrived. We went back into the classroom 20-30 minutes later and we looked out the window only to see an ambulance truck carrying my 5th grade teacher away. After that, the rest of the school day was a blur, but I do remember telling my mom what happened and she was beyond surprised.

I also said:

"I hope he doesn't go into that big classroom in the sky!"

That's when she said:

"Everything will be all right! Mr. Dan's going to be fine."

Later that day as I got ready to go to bed, I got down on my knees on the edge of the bed and prayed for Mr. Dan.

I said:

"Dear Lord, thank you for this day and thank you for the blessings that you have bestowed upon me . . . . God, I want you to take care of Mr. Dan. I want you to make him better again because I miss him. Amen."

The next day when I went to school and walked into my classroom . . . *there he was!* I went over to his desk and asked him what happened.

He said:

"My doctor told me that I needed to watch my cholesterol and that I need to have a healthy diet."

At that point, I realized what the phrase "Life is short" meant. Mr. Dan could've died yesterday and then what? We wouldn't have a teacher. That was one of the most infamous moments that I've ever experienced in my life. That's why I am truly blessed to have a role model like Mr. Dan in my life because without him, part of me wouldn't exist.

Another thing that I remember was when I met Valerie Rodriguez. She was a gorgeous and beautiful girl that blew my mind! In the beginning, we were cool, but then she didn't like me. I mean, I couldn't even have a friendly conversation with her. I tried so hard to be a good friend to her every chance that I get, but she would always say:

"Leave me alone!" or "Get away from me!" I remember one day she had on a black shirt that said in white lettering:

{Anything boys can do, girls can do better!}

Then after I finished reading it, she said in an obnoxious tone:

"And it's true!"

I just wanted to have a conversation with her, but it turns out that I couldn't even get two words out. I don't know why, but I try so hard to be a good friend only to get shot down. I wanted to have a lot of friends, but now I know it's better to have a faithful few than a fake flock. Like my mom would always say "Less is more". I realized something about girls and that is, they will never be satisfied and in their mind, they are always right.

Another thing that I remember was meeting a boy named Darrell. Darrell was the type of person that understood my weirdness and plays along. He was fun to hang out with and was well-liked. I was the main person that he hung out with because we were the exact same person. We understood each other, we hung out with each other, and he was a very smart person. He kind of reminds me of a friend that I have **right now**. (Only he knows who I'm talking about).

Anyway, I remember that it was the last day that he was going to be at this school. For the remainder of the time we had together, we pretty much did our thing and talked about whatever was on our minds trying to create some sort of wacky scenario that we could play along with. Then, he had this red mechanical pencil. This red mechanical pencil had a soft, spiral grip on the base of the pencil and I just took it. Darrell came back to his table, saw his pencil wasn't on the table and automatically said to me:

"Give me my pencil."

I looked at him and said:

"I didn't take your pencil."

Darrell looked at me sternly and said:

"I'm not playing with you, man. Give me my pencil."

I looked at him, with a wide grin on my face and said:

"I don't have your pencil, man."

I was laughing and talking at the same time even though he could tell that I was lying, but didn't want to create a scene.

Darrell looked at me one more time and said:

"Come on, man. Please give me back my pencil!"

I looked back at him, laughing as hard as I could and said to him:

"I don't have your pencil, Darrell."

I couldn't believe what I just did. I lied to my best friend right in his face. When I look back at this moment in time, I feel mortally wounded because I took something that my friend desperately needed and lied to him about having it. That's mainly one of the ways on how I lose good friends and when you lose them, you find out the value that they had on your life. That's why you shouldn't lie because there's absolutely no point in lying.

Cherish real friends and treat them with care because you never know when you may lose them. Also, it's never okay to lie to someone esp. if it's someone who you want to be in your life.

Chapter 4

---◦❋◦---

Sixth grade. Boy, do I have something to say about sixth grade! Sixth grade was supposed to be a new journey. A wonderful adventure. I have left the crybabies behind and I was on to bigger and better things. But there was only one problem . . . bullies! It all started when I attended Hill Valley Middle School.

When I went to Hill Valley Middle School, the one thing that I noticed was that some kids that went to Ocean Way with me went to Hill Valley Middle School too. Another thing that I noticed was all the sixth, seventh, and eighth grade halls were all painted in different colors. The 6th grade hall was painted blue, the 7th grade hall was painted yellow and the 8th grade hall was painted red. Another thing that I also noticed was that there were a lot of bright and smiling faces hugging each other and welcoming each other back to school. But just because everything looked like a rainbow doesn't mean there was a pot of gold at the end of it. I had a lot of good and bad experiences at this school that I will never forget.

For example, I was always the main target for bullying. I was constantly being bullied by a whole bunch of people for different types of reasons. For example, I was bullied by this one dude who had a locker that was underneath my locker. He was always being mean to me every time I would try to say something to him and I really didn't know why. It was like every time I would be at my locker; he would always be saying things like "Move!" or something else. I told my mom about the situation and she said:

"Just tell him to give you a minute at opening your locker!"

And that's exactly what I did. When I went to school the next day, I went to my locker, opened my locker and guess who came behind me? That's right! The **bully!** He said:

"I need to get to my locker!"

I said:

"Give me a minute!"

I opened my locker, got my materials for Math class and left, but before I did I asked him something.

I asked, nervously:

"Why are you bullying me?"

He said:

"I don't know."

I said:

"Well, I didn't do anything to you, man."

He said:

"OK, I'm sorry for messing with you. I was just playing around."

Then he extended his hand and I shook it. That was the moment that I was cool with a bully or at least gotten everything settled. He got the materials that he needed for his next class, closed his bottom locker and hit his head on the bottom part of my top locker. That was the last time that I seen him or remembered seeing him ever, but that wouldn't be the last time that I would be bullied.

Another thing that I remember was when I got bullied by a girl named Shannon Crossly. Shannon was the type of girl that was trying to get everyone in the world to see that she was the smartest and the baddest chick in the building. I mean, when it came to Shannon, there was never a time where she didn't bully me. The one thing that she would tease me on was the fact that I had buck teeth because every day I would see her, she would always call me "Bucky" every time. Either that or some ridiculous name that had the word "buck" in it. If she wasn't doing that, the group of girls that she always had with her would be teasing me and there wouldn't be anything that I could do about it.

Another thing that I remember was that this time, I wasn't getting bullied by one person, but two girls at the same exact time. Megan Coleman and Damica Knox. I was getting bullied by these two girls for absolutely no reason whatsoever! These girls just knew how to get under my skin. They would curse at me, yell at me, treat me wrong, call me "ugly", the whole nine yards. These girls had to be the most ghetto bunch of girls that I ever been around. I mean, I even had classes with these girls, so you already knew that the bullying was constant and non-stop! It never seemed to die until I went my way and they went theirs.

But then, there was the bully that ended the camel's life. He was the most ignorant person that ever walked the halls of Hill Valley Middle School. His name was Drago Callus. Drago was like the 'Deebo' of middle school because he would always try to mess with me every chance he'd get. Plus, every time I would try to stand my ground against him, it was as if he had mind control over me because I couldn't do anything about whatever he did towards me. I felt helpless against him like a child that's being abused by another person. He always made fun of me by calling me "crocodile mouth" because my teeth were crooked. He would also have a group of boys to back him up whenever he was messing with me. They had his back everywhere he went just like Shannon and her group of girls. They were like his army that served him and were always loyal to him. I mean, I was so upset that he was treating me like this that I had to switch classes and even then, things didn't get better.

When I switched classes, it turned out to be the worst decision that we ever decided to do because I got bullied in my class. I got teased by the same group of boys that followed Drago around. They picked on me, they made fun of the way I talked, and they, like all the great bullies in this world, tried to get inside my head.

If you thought that was rough, just listen to what happened in my newly assigned last class of the day. In my last class, it was horrible because the entire class was being rebellious against my teacher. That's when my teacher got as mad as she could at all the kids in her classroom and I actually started to cry. It hurt so bad to watch one of my favorite teachers lash out at the entire class all because they chose to disrespect her. It was like I was a little kid watching his father get beat up or something like that. That's when I went to the office and got my schedule switched back to the way it was.

You may've thought that when I got my schedule changed that everything was all fine and dandy, right? Then if you thought that, you're dead wrong. I mean, I didn't have to deal with all the people that I had to deal with before, but I still had some problems. One day when I went to gym class, this dude was trying to get inside my head by teasing me. And if that's not enough, this big dude was also teasing me while I was trying to open my locker by dancing behind me. That's when I screamed from the top of my lungs in rage ready to kill him because I had it up to here with the bull crap that everyone was giving me! That's when I talked to my mom about the pain that I was suffering and she came up with a plan. She created something called the "Bully List."

The Bully List was specifically designed to write down any bully's name that's been giving me problems and report it to my mom and that's just what I did. From then on, if I ever had any problems with a bully, then I would just write their name down and report it. Having a paper trail was the best way to prove what was going on and they had to listen to me then and my mom made them. After that, nobody ever messed with me again. Now, this is where my good experiences come in.

The 1ˢᵗ good experience that I had in that school was meeting my best friend Calvin. Calvin was the type of person that was fun to be around and he was one of the main people that I would hang with. It was like we were Cheech and Chong, Kenan and Kel, Starsky and Hutch, Drake and Josh, etc. We always hung out together at all times and we always had each other's back. I mean, I had friends at that school, but none of them came close to *my friend*. He made 6ᵗʰ grade memorable for me in all the things that we did. From being in paper ball wars to throwing airplanes in the back of the classroom without being seen, we'd always have fun with each other. I even hung out with Calvin on my birthday. On my birthday, my mom drove to his house, picked him up and we drove to the movies to see *The Game Plan*. I not only saw the movie with Calvin, but with my cousin and my other friend Seth. That day was a good day because I was with people that actually **wanted** to be around me and I couldn't have wished it any other way. It's people like Calvin that made life worth living. He, along with all the other friends that I had in the past, made it possible for me to be myself without being criticized by a judgmental society. That's why Calvin will hold a special place in my heart.

My 2ⁿᵈ good experience that I had in that school was when I met another friend that made me see the value that adults have for the next generation. He made me feel like I was the most brilliant person within a 50 mile radius. I seem to have that effect on most adults because only adults seem to see the intelligence that I had to offer while other kids had to be incredibly smart to understand what I was saying.

William Cartier had to be the most caring individual that I've ever known besides my mom. I mean, it's because of that calm demeanor that got him a great family, great friends and the perfect job that seem to fit all of his calmness and patience all into one place. He was the school's guidance counselor and the highlight of my days in that school. Every morning of every day or every time that I had permission, I would always go to his office and talk to him, play games with him and just have fun with him. He also listened to me and always seemed to analyze the myriad of knowledge that I revealed towards him. I would not only tell him the things about me, but also go on and on and on about Michael Jackson. I would always talk to him about Michael Jackson. My favorite song by him, a Michael Jackson music video that I would see over the weekend, the fact that I would like to wear his glove, his hat, everything. If not Michael Jackson, then Michael J. Fox and how much I love the *Back to the Future Trilogy* and the movie *Teen Wolf.* Oh My Gosh, of all the times I would talk about Michael J. Fox! I would always talk to him about the flux capacitor, Marty McFly, Doc Emmett Brown, Einstein, or the Delorean time machine itself. I would always go on for hours and hours on end about Back to the Future or Teen Wolf. Mr. Cartier and I even tried to create our own story that involved the Michael J. Fox from Back to the Future and the Michael J. Fox from Teen Wolf. It had something to do with both of them switching lives where the Michael J. Fox from Back to the Future was the Michael J. Fox from Teen Wolf and how the Michael J. Fox from Teen Wolf was the Michael J. Fox from Back to the Future. You see how I can go on and on, right?! It was just us expressing our love for the classics. That's the type of relationship that I wanted to have with people instead of a relationship of rejection and hate. I want a relationship with a person that doesn't end in the words "I hate you and I never want to see you again!" I want a relationship with people where I won't have to always be excluded from a group. I want a relationship with people that share exquisite interests in things that I can relate to and have unique insights on life without having to fake it. I want to have a relationship one day with a girl that sees me for the wondrous intellect that I have to offer and the passionate side that I have. I want to have a relationship with people that don't feel threatened by me. I want to have a relationship with people where they understand me for who I am. That's the type of people that I want to be around and that's why Mr. Cartier played a key role in my middle school experience. It was him that listened to my thoughts and feelings on things that I felt were important. It was him that switched me from a bad situation into a new one because he knew that I was in dire need of a change. He is what made my time in Hill Valley Middle School memorable. He is who I gladly like to call a *friend.*

Choose your friends wisely.
* Make the best out of a bad situation. It's up to you to stand up and fight back against the oppressors of the world!*
You are in control of your destiny!

Chapter 5

—•❀•—

Now I may have had something to say about 6th grade, but it wasn't as bad as 7th. At least that's how it was in the beginning of 7th grade because it got better as I went down the road. It all started when I attended Laruso Magnet Academy in Georgia.

The main reason that I went to Laruso was the exact same reason that I went to Hill Valley: I thought my friend was going to be there. When I first got there, I saw how old the building was and how it looked ancient and practically dilapidated. At least, that was my opinion. I walked into my homeroom class and met my homeroom teacher who would also be my 2nd period math teacher Mr. Douglass. Mr. Douglass was an African—American male in his mid or late 30s that was a highly educated individual who was bald. He may have been an interesting person to be around, but the way that he taught Math . . . not so interesting. As he was introducing himself, I was gazing out the door of his classroom only to find my friend that I wanted to go to school with walking in a line with another group of students. I waved at him hoping he would see me, but he didn't. His name was Michael and I knew Michael since kindergarten. We were childhood friends and he was the one that wanted me to go to that school so badly. Now that we got Michael straightened out, back to me!

The one thing that I noticed was that I saw another group of people that I went to Ocean Way Elementary School with. It's been *years* since I seen these people! I was absolutely impressed at the number of people that I saw at that school that I knew in the past. I figured that I was going to fit in perfectly with the people at this school. It's practically memory lane!

The only problem was there were some people in my homeroom class that I didn't get along with. For example, there was this boy who was smaller than I was that had a problem with me for no reason whatsoever. He wasn't friendly at all. My goal was to make new friends, but this boy was making it hard for me to do so. That's when I avoided him the best way I could, but then he started messing with me! I mean, what did I ever do to him? I didn't even know him, but he was giving me problems. He was giving me problems in homeroom, Gym, Math, Science, even Art. But then something happened that blew all of that drama out of the water.

One day in Gym class, he collapsed because he hurt his leg. That's when I sprang into action and helped him up. Now when I did this, it was a sign that I had a willingness to forgive and forget all of the things that he put me through in order to make amends. I put his arm around my neck and acted as a crutch to him. He saw the heroic effort that I was trying to give and knew that "I came in peace". I carried him all the way to the bleachers and sat him down.

I asked him:

"Are you OK?"

He said:

"Yeah."

That's when I realized that since I got him talking now; I could probably start a conversation.

I asked him:

"Do you watch *Family Guy?*"

He said:

"Yeah. Did you see the chicken fight last night?"

I said:

"Yeah! It was the 3rd one!"

That's when something magical happened! We became friends at that moment. I finally got someone on my side. Someone who I can talk to. Someone who I can hang with without there being any problems. Someone who I can have good times with. It was a good moment that I didn't expect to happen, but since it did, I was alright.

Another thing that I remember from Laruso was that girls are not all made of sugar and spice. There are some girls that have bricks or coal for hearts and tongues that spit fire. Case in point, Alice and Stacy. Stacy was a girl that was mean to me for no reason. It's like every time Stacy saw me, she would always call me "Ugly", "Nasty" and saying "Shut Up" to me. She was just straight up obnoxious to me. I mean, she even made fun of the way that I talk. I would always get words jumbled up and I could barely even say a complete sentence when I spoke. I spoke like that since I was little and she, along with other people in the past, would always make fun of my speech impediment. Alice was Stacy's cosigner. Everything Stacy did, Alice would back up. If Stacy talked about my clothes, Alice would talk about my hair and shoes. This was an everyday occurrence. But that's not how Alice was in the beginning.

Alice made everything feel alright and that's when I wanted to "be around" her. I mean, she was the most beautiful, smartest, and nicest girl that I ever seen. The thing about her is there were times where we would have good conversations and times where we would get sour with one another. That's what would happen with Alice and me at times. That's what happens with me and a whole bunch of other people in my life. That's one of the main problems that I have when I try to make friends. It's the same old thing. Jaylon meets friend, Jaylon does something wrong, friendship with friend is broken. Then when I try to get them to take me back into their lives, they won't let me back in and when they do, I mess up again for some odd reason. That's honestly one of the reasons why at times when I mess up, I want to be alone so I wouldn't have to worry about other people and making them upset.

Another thing that I remember from Laruso wasn't even funny at all. It was downright cruel, disrespectful and straight up evil. One day, I got permission from my last period teacher to go to the bathroom. I went to the bathroom and just when I walked into the stall, another boy saw me. He immediately walked towards me, put his hands around my neck and choked me. I was trying to get him off of my neck, but he had his hands wrapped around my neck pretty tight. That's when he released his hands from my neck and walked away. I was hurt and sad that someone would want to choke me like that out of the blue for no reason. I left the bathroom, went to my classroom, told my teacher what happened in the bathroom and she told me to write it up. I went into my notebook, ripped out a piece of paper, wrote down everything that happened in the bathroom and gave it to her. She said that she was going to report it to the office and they will handle the situation. To be honest, in all of my years of being alive, I never thought that being choked by another human being for no reason whatsoever would ever happen to me in my life unless I were to physically harm another person. Other than that, why? I never felt so helpless, so weak, and so afraid to retaliate. It took me back to when I was at Bayside Elementary and I hit my classmate. I didn't retaliate because I never wanted to feel like I felt back then. I didn't want to get in trouble like that again. So that's why I did nothing at that moment.

Another thing that I remember was when I asked Mr. Douglass if I could go to the bathroom. He let me go to the bathroom and I left the class. I walked down the hallway to go to the bathroom when I saw my friend Amanda talking to this dark-skinned girl. Here's where things got real! She saw me walk down the hall and she said to her:

"Girl, you know he's ugly!"

That's when I stopped, turned around and told her:

"Shut up!"

That's when she came out and started talking junk about me, but I don't remember what she said. I just remember me putting my hand in her face signifying that "I don't care about the garbage that comes out of your mouth." That's when she removed my hand from my face and the next thing I know both of us were going at it. She kept pulling my hoodie over my head, so I couldn't see anything. That's when she picked my head up and she repeatedly slammed it against a locker. That's when I got her and I rammed her into a locker. All of a sudden, some teachers came out of their classrooms, saw us going at it, and broke us up. That's when I was sent to the office and they called my parents. My mom came up to the school, mad as heck, and my principal suspended me for 3 days.

My mom gave me the "business" in the car and for the remainder of the 3 days that I was suspended; I was told that I had to do work around the house. You know, rake leaves, wash dishes, clean the house, that type of stuff. I guess that's what happens when you make bad decisions in life. And then there was this.

The last thing that I did was by far the most idiotic thing that I could've done in my life; I told a joke *to a teacher.* To be frank, when I told this joke, I didn't expect this type of reaction to happen, but I might as well tell you how it all started. I was leaving Language Arts class one day to go to Science class, but first I had to go to my locker. I got my Science folder and my Science book and walked to class. As I walked down the hall, I saw Mrs. Marley by her door. I went to Mrs. Marley and I started talking to Mrs. Marley about whatever was on my mind. We were laughing, we were smiling, we were having a good time with the conversation that we were having. Then I decided to bring a joke into the conversation and that's when I said the most unnecessary, dumbest and practically immoral thing that I could ever say. It was so stupid that if a time machine was invented, I would go back to the year 1995 and tell my mom to have an abortion on me. The joke that I said was:

"If I was crazy enough, I would come to the school and kill everyone!"

To this day, every time I think about that day, I hold my head down in utter disappointment, embarrassment and humiliation, but back to the story. When I said that, me and Mrs. Marley laughed, but then she did something peculiar. She told the teacher, whose class I was just about to enter, what I just said to her and that's when things got jacked up. Then Mrs. Marley called me over to her and that's when she told me that I was going to the office.

I said, nervously:

"What?!! What did I do?"

She said:

"Jaylon, you can't say things like that in school!"

I got nervous as heck and said:

"But you knew that I was joking! You knew that I was playing!"

That's when out of the blue, my principal was walking down the hall and Mrs. Marley told her everything that happened. That's when she escorted me straight to the office and I was crying while I was going to the office. They had me sit down in this conference room and that's where I remained for 1 or 2 hours. The entire time that I was there, I was nervous, I was sad and I would repeatedly say the phrase "It wasn't meant to be taken literally!" every time someone would ask me why I said what I said. The vice principal wanted to see me in her office to hear my side of the story. I wrote down everything that happened followed by the phrase "It wasn't meant to be taken literally." Later, someone came into the room and asked me if I ate lunch or not. I said:

"No."

The office let me leave the room to have lunch and they even let me eat the lunch in the room. Even the food didn't make me feel better about the situation that I was in. That's when I saw my dad walking into the office and I got severely nervous. I was called back into the vice principal's office, so someone could tell me something.

I asked:

"What's going on?"

My dad said, calmly:

"You won't be going to this school anymore, Jaylon. So pack everything!

That's when I felt like the most blithering idiot on the face of the earth. I went to my locker, got my things and just when I was about to leave, Mrs. Marley suddenly want to speak to me.

"Jaylon, I apologize for what happened. I didn't mean to make it like this."

That's when I gave her a look that said "Are you serious? You didn't think something like this was going to happen?!!"

I said:

"Mrs. Marley, you knew that I was joking, but you told on me anyway!"

That's when my social studies teacher, Mr. Addleman, asked what was going on. I didn't feel like telling the entire story, so I just said:

"I'm leaving."

He said:

"Well, have a nice life!"

That's when I got all of my things, closed my locker and left the building. When I got home, that's when I got the "business" from my dad and went to sleep. The next day, we went to the Administration Office so I could be assigned a new school. Where I was going next made me understand the true meaning of the phrase "It gets better."

Make your haters your motivators and don't do the stupid things that I did.
* Learn from my mistakes and don't continue to make the same mistakes over and over. Because then, you haven't learned anything.*

Chapter 6

————————•◦✦◦•————————

The next school that I went to for the remainder of my 7th grade year was called East Lawndale Middle School. It was a school in Georgia that focused on gifted and talented kids. It was considered to be the best middle school in the city. When I walked into the building, I had to wait an hour and a half for the staff to get me straightened out. After I was a part of their school, I had to go to the library to get my picture taken for my ID card. Once I did that, I was officially a student of East Lawndale Middle School.

The way East Lawndale did things when it came to where our classes would be played out a bit differently. Instead of running all over the building trying to get from one class to another, we would go in a circle. That meant that the same people that you have homeroom with are the same people that will be in all of your classes. At first, I didn't know anyone who went to school at East Lawndale, so I was by myself. My homeroom teacher, Mrs. Molly, was pretty much always nice to me every day. I mean, anytime that I asked for help, she didn't want me to hesitate. She was one of the sweetest and most beautiful teachers that I had at that school and she really knew how to make me feel welcome. I mean, I never seen her get upset with anyone over anything! Ever! Almost as if she was immune to anger. She would get irritated, but she wouldn't get angry. That's why I will always love Mrs. Molly.

Another thing that I remember from 7th grade was when I met Dre' Walker. Dre Walker was a boy that always seemed to pick me as his target because everything that I do, he would always have something to say about it.

Every move that I'd make, he would always have something to say about it. He would always tease me and call me out every chance that he would get. If I sat in front of him, he'd kick my seat. If I was in front of him in a certain line, he'd tap me and pretend he didn't do it. That's when I thought of a plan! Retaliation! Do to him what he did to me! And that's exactly what I did. Whenever I was sitting behind him, I was kicking his seat. If he was behind me in line and he tapped me, I'd hit him back. The only problem with that was he would be the victim and *I* would be the bully which was the complete opposite of how the story went. That's when I was the one getting into trouble and he wasn't. No one wanted to listen to my side, but ***everyone*** wanted to listen to his story. That's what ticks me off, when you aren't being fair and you treat me like I'm the bad guy. That's why I prefer to be alone most of the time because people are foolish enough to believe anything even when it's a ***bold-faced lie.*** I even remember trying to peel off my own skin because my teacher called my parents and told them the complete opposite of what really happened. Then, my dad came to the school and listened to every word that my teacher told him. Now, both of my parents were mad at me and refused to believe anything that I said. That's when I learned that when you fight back against people, it's pointless. It doesn't solve anything and all it does is make matters worse when it could've easily been avoidable. I guess that's why in this game, there was really one winner and one loser and I apparently lost. Well played, Dre. Well played indeed.

Another thing that I remember was when I met Ms. Trenton. Ms. Trenton was an art teacher that taught not only art, but chess. She was the main person that taught me how to play chess and I was one of her favorite students. It wasn't because of my smile or anything; it was because she admired my creativity, my curiosity, and my intelligence. That's something that I don't think too many people would pay attention to. I was glad to have had at least one person notice that than a million people who could care less about it. To me, it was better than nobody caring at all. I remember my 1st assignment was to color a dragon that she drew. The dragon looked like a dragon that you would see on the cover of *Eragon, or Harry Potter and the Goblet of Fire* because it looked spectacular beyond comprehension. To this day, I still have that dragon picture hanging on my wall. She not only drew that, but she drew a bunch of other things that looked like they should be placed in a museum. That's why I told her one day, she should display her art work for the entire world to see. I remember that she loved my intelligence so much that she gave me her own books from her personal shelf entitled *How Things Work*. It was an honor to be given that book because she never gave anything to anybody. (At least, not to my knowledge).

The relationship that I had with Ms. Trenton reminded me of the relationship that I had with Mr. Cartier. She understood me as a person and saw me for the divine qualities that I possess. In her eyes, I was a man with good intentions and a love for being myself. I just wish there were more people in this world like Ms. Trenton.

Another thing that I remember was meeting my brand new teacher Mrs. Berry. Mrs. Berry was my Language Arts teacher in 7th grade. The one thing that I would remember was the warmth that her classroom had every time you'd walk into it each and every day. It was cozy and it felt like home. It felt real good. I remember lying on the wall and sinking straight to the floor with a big, wide grin on my face. If you were to see what I looked like when I chilled on the floor, you'd think I was high. Then there was Mrs. Berry. Mrs. Berry had to be one of the coolest teachers that I had in 7th grade. She believed in making her lessons fun and engaging. I don't remember one time where Mrs. Berry ever made us fall asleep in her class plus she was a very smart person.

For example, we had a preposition test or a spelling test or something like that the next day. She wanted us to memorize this very long list of words by tomorrow, so what I did was I wrote all of the words down on a sheet of loose leaf paper planning to use it on the test. (Yes, even me! As smart as I am! Actually tried to cheat on a spelling exam!) The next day when the big day came, Mrs. Berry said:

"Alright! I want a pen or pencil and a clean sheet of paper on top of your desk now."

That's when I went into my folder, pulled out the cheat sheet and put it on my desk. I waited until she said "Start the test" but instead she said:

"Alright! Hand over your cheat sheets!"

In my head, I was thinking "What the flip? How did she know?" I was utterly shocked yet impressed. It wasn't often that I would run across a teacher that was clever enough to spot my tricks. That was one of the moments that I remember when she demonstrated her wit to me and I realized she's pretty hard to fool. I also remember when she first gave us our Language Arts book and she wanted us to call it our "Academic Bible" because we would always bring it to class every time we would come into her class. One time, I actually forgot to bring my book into class and she didn't even notice. It was just a book that we would work out of whenever we were instructed to do so. You know, for work and stuff.

The one thing that Mrs. Berry was known for, in my opinion, was making the class realize that every class in the world shouldn't be boring unless you make it boring. That's one of the things that made me love Mrs. Berry each and every day of 7ᵗʰ grade.

Another thing that I remember from 7ᵗʰ grade was when I met my friend Trent Avery. Trent was the type of person that played by his own rules and did things that he thought were cool. He would say what was on his mind and do what was on his mind. Now, if you were to meet Trent and see him, you'd probably think that he did something wrong like kill a man or something because he always had a menacing look on his face. It made him look evil even though he wasn't. He was actually a pretty smart person with a two-sided personality. He likes *Batman, Star Wars, Indiana Jones, Harry Potter, & Pirates of the Caribbean.* Man, did he love talking about Pirates of the Caribbean! He would go for hours on end talking about how great Jack Sparrow is, how he'd wish he could own his sword, and how he'd wish to fight side by side with Captain Jack Sparrow. I mean, he loved Pirates of the Caribbean so much that he would play Pirates of the Caribbean games on his PC and his PS3. If he wasn't playing Lego Pirates of the Caribbean on his PS3, then he would be playing Pirates of the Caribbean on his desktop computer. He would spend hours on Pirates of the Caribbean Online going from one island to another to explore new places, meet new people and find hidden treasures. If he wasn't talking about Pirates of the Caribbean, he would talk about Star Wars and if he wasn't talking about Star Wars, he would talk about DragonBall Z. If not that, he would talk about Naruto and the list goes on and on and on.

The reason that I liked hanging out with Trent was because he was never afraid to be himself plus he was always fun to be around. It's like when I'm around Trent, the phrase "Don't judge a book by its cover" really takes a toll on me. If you knew Trent and saw him, you'd see a man that looked like he was depressed about life, but when you get to know him, you'd understand that he's very special in his own unique way. That's honestly why to this day; he will always be one of my friends that I hold near and dear to my heart.

When you meet new people, see them for who they are and find the value in those people.
When confronted by a "bully", pay them no mind. They should mean nothing to you.
Instead, ask yourself "What is going on in their lives that would make them want to be mad at me?"

Chapter 7

───────── ·•❈•· ─────────

8th grade is finally here! It was the best of times, it was the worst of times! It made me take a look at the world around me and made me see that my environment was far from safe. It also made me realize the true meaning of the phrase "Everything happens for a reason". 8th grade also gave me 3 of the closest friends that I ever had and it all started at East Lawndale Middle School.

I decided to come back to ELMS that year for the following reasons:

One

It was closer to my house

Two

I knew a whole lot of people there now

Three

It was a good place to go to school

In 8th grade, I remember having good and bad experiences throughout my school year. I remember meeting new teachers and facing new obstacles along the way. I also remember meeting the only 3 people that I would be spending every single minute of my scholastic school year with. They were my best friends and also my main friends that I would have at the school. My 1st friend was Corey Bradford. Corey was the boy at school that said what was on his mind, criticized the harsh reality that we lived in just like I did and played by his own rules at all times. He loves *The Boondocks, South Park, video games, girls, etc.* He told me things about himself that I didn't even know and it made me see a different side of him that I didn't know could be manifested. Corey and I were the only 2 people that truly connected with each other. I mean, we would talk about anything. We would talk about *Naruto, Shonen Jump, our lives, the cruel and unruly injustices of the world, people in general, anything.* I remember always letting him read my *Game Informer magazines* because he loves to read them. One time, he saw an article talking about the new *Pokémon* game and he ripped the entire page out of my magazine! Another thing that I remember was this time where we started talking about Shaq and we had a debate on whether he was a rapper or not. He still doesn't believe me when I say he is. All and all, he was one of my best friends that I had in 8th grade.

Another friend that I had was named Will Thompson. Will was the type of person that went to school, did his work, got along with everyone and didn't get into trouble. I remember that Will and I were always competing with each other and it would be over simple things like:

- Who was more intelligent
- Who knew the most girls
- Who had the best grades?

We even competed to see who Corey liked hanging out with more. It was just us going back and forth and back and forth at each other. As I look back at all of that, it was dumb. I mean, what was the point? Even if I was the most intelligent, knew the most girls, and hung out with Corey more, who would care? No one! Another thing that I remember about Will was that he always showed favoritism, mostly to girls. When it came to girls, Will would always be quick to give girls a million dollars if he had it. Will always had candy on his person and whenever I would ask for candy, he wouldn't give me candy. But when one girl asked for one piece of candy, he'd start giving candy to people then! That's what I didn't like about Will because nobody likes a person that plays favorites, but now I understand that he loved the girls! I remember one time, he brought a gold chain to school. It was a gold money bag with a green dollar sign in the middle of the bag. Man, it was a nice chain! I would've liked to own one myself if I knew where he got it from.

Anyway, he brought it to school one day and another student wanted to wear it. He let him wear it and later in the day, it was gone. Now Will didn't have a chain, but guess who he blamed for losing it! Not me, but Corey! He blamed Corey out of all people and Corey was nowhere near the chain! Will would always turn against his friends whenever something went wrong in his life. He was a fair weather friend, only nice when things are going his way.

Now, my 3rd friend had to be the funniest person that I was happy to be around. He may have been slow in class, but he was my friend all the same. His name was Monty Borroughs. Monty was a person that was funny, funny-looking and he was cool to be around. He was also unorganized, messy and overweight. I remember every time we would get an assignment in class, it would take him a long time for him to get finished with that one assignment. When it came to Monty, it was as if time slowed down for him because it would take him 10 minutes to write one sentence on a writing assignment and probably 1 hour to write one paragraph. Me, Corey, and Will would try to help him with his work, but it seems as if he wants to do things on his own. Another thing that I remember about Monty was he was real messy. He had papers from classes just stuffed into his folders and everything was crumbled up.

Everything that Monty had was messed up! Folders, workbooks, assignments, scratch paper, etc. I mean, Monty was so trashy that he had his own personal junkyard in his room! I remember Will told me that he went to his house one day to spend the night and the 1st thing he talked about was his room. He talked about how there were clothes, shoes, socks, and junk all over his room. To me, it was just a disaster to see someone live that way and think it's okay! I'm surprised he wasn't on *Hoarders!* You put all 3 of them together and you had my friends, but there were times where we didn't see eye to eye with each other.

For example, I remember going to lunch every day and we would always argue at our table. There was never a time where we didn't argue

51

at our table and it would be over anything. We'd argue over who owed people money, Will's favoritism towards girls, one of us failing to do any work in class or even my intelligence. Corey would always get mad at me because I knew more than him and he resorted to calling me a "know-it-all." I mean, that was just a little bit off the deep end. I can't help how smart I am and it's my job to actually *become smart*. I don't know if he was jealous or anything because I knew more than him or if he was trying to get me off of my game, but I was never going to stop being smart. It's just who I am and if no one likes it, *you don't have to be around me!*

To me, it's like the more we argued, the more we began to hate each other. It then turned into something that we would do every time we would sit down at lunch and we would talk about the same thing. It would have us laughing, upset, and even in complete and utter silence. But hey, it's what we did! Dysfunction at its best, but it worked for us.

Another thing that I remember was when Corey made a group called the A.B. Crew. The A.B. Crew was inspired off of trying to do better on our report cards because we wanted As and Bs. That's pretty much where the A.B. came in. I mean, it wasn't a gang or anything. It was just our group of friends in school that wanted to start a group. It was an "us" thing. The group's sole members were Corey, Monty, Will, and Yours Truly.

Then, we were trying to figure out what type of group it would be. That's when it became a group on *Facebook*. I created the Facebook group and that's what it is to this day. I mean, this group meant something to me. It was the 1st group that I was actually a part of. It wasn't a group that I was immediately excluded from because of who I was. It wasn't a group that made me feel less than a person. It was a group that made me feel like an actual human being and that's all that I wanted from everyone. Equality . . . and I been denied that from so many people so many times that the only way that I could walk hand and hand with another person is if they were my brother or sister. That's what the A.B. Crew meant to me and that's what it's always going to mean. The 1st time I felt truly accepted as an equal.

Another thing that I remember was when I met a beautiful girl. This girl had to be the most gorgeous girl in the entire building *and there were some beautiful women in that building.* I wanted to be that girl's one and only because she was so fine that she took Miss America's place! The 1st time that I went to speak to her was when I drew a heart for her in class. My teacher was going over the Holocaust and showing the film adaptation of the book *The Diary of Anne Frank.* I felt that if I didn't do something like this for her, then she'll never know how I feel about her and I was gaga over her! I would have dreams about her and I being together and loving each other in so many different possible ways! It was just insane! When class was over, I met her in the hallway and said to her:

"I made this for you. It's just to show you how I feel about you."

She smiled and said:

"Aw, thank you!"

She walked away to her class and I watched her walk all the way to her class, thinking:

"What does a guy like me have to do to get a girl like that?"

All throughout math class, all I could think about was her and all the things she could be doing to that one drawing. She could be ripping it up right now as we speak. She could've balled it up and threw it in the trash. She could've done a lot of things to it that I'd never expect to happen. That's why I hoped and prayed that she didn't do any of the things to that sheet of paper. When class was over, I went inside of her class to see her and she was drop dead gorgeous. She had on a gray shirt with short shorts. *Oh my gosh*, she was **ridiculously fine**! She took a picture with her class and they all left. I followed her and asked her:

"Do you need some help carrying your stuff?"

She said:

"No, I got it. I'm a strong girl."

That when I wanted to know how she felt about the picture, so I asked:

"So, did you like my picture?"

She said:

"It was sweet."

That's when I went my way out of the school and she went out through the back door, getting on her bus.

The next day when I went to school, I saw her again in homeroom. I was so excited to see her in class that my nervous system shut down. As I sat down in a desk that was by her, I couldn't help but think that I was missing something . . . Oh yeah! Her name! I don't know her name! When the bell rang, I talked to her and asked her:

"What's your name?"

She said:

"Mary."

I said:

"That's a beautiful name."

She said:

"Thank you!"

Well, what a coincidence! Her name was Mary and that's exactly what I wanted to do with her! The bad thing about this entire thing was that the only time I would see her is when I'm at lunch and in homeroom. That's it. I had no classes with Mary meaning that time was not on my side. Also, after that day, she wasn't at school for a couple of days. That's when I felt slightly irritated inside. I had thoughts of what her sudden absence could mean. Maybe she got hurt and it was a serious injury. Maybe she got sick. Maybe she got into an accident. But I didn't think too much of it. When she finally came back a week later, I went to her, excitedly and said:

"Hey, Mary. Where have you been? I missed you!"

She said:

"Aw, that's so sweet. I was helping my mom with some things."

I said:

"Oh."

That's when everything went back to the way they were supposed to until 9/11. When 9/11 came, everything for me shut down. Not because of what happened in New York and the Pentagon, but what happened in my middle school. On 9/11, I walked into the school building only to see Mary and she looked absolutely stunning beyond belief. For one thing, all she had on was a ruby red dress. When I saw her in that dress, my jaw dropped all the way to the ground. I mean, she looked good enough to be in a modeling picture surrounded by a million red roses.

Anyway, later in the day, there was an assembly that was about 9/11 and the horrific loss of all the victims involved in that tragic moment. Mary happened to be one of the speakers of the presentation. I wasn't even paying attention to what anybody else said. I was just waiting for her to speak because her voice sounded like angels singing. When she went to the podium, I stood up in my seat and listened to every last word as if it would be the last time I would hear her ever again. When she was done, I clapped as hard as I could for her just to show my appreciation towards her.

After the assembly was over, I got the most heartbreaking news that I could ever receive. (Besides Michael Jackson's passing). I looked inside my Science teacher's classroom only to find people telling Mary things like "Good Bye", "We'll miss you" and "I hope you meet lots of new people!". I asked my Science teacher what was going on and she told me that she was moving to Maryland. What another coincidence! Her name is Mary and she's moving to Maryland! That's when I went over to her and asked her:

"You're leaving?

She said:

"Yeah. I'm moving to Maryland."

That's when I hugged her and didn't let go even when people tried to pull me off of her. I said:

"I can't believe you're leaving! Even though I knew you for a couple of days!"

She said:

"No, you didn't. You knew me for a year!"

As I was hugging her, I remember in 7th grade year, I told her that she looked beautiful when we were at a school fair, so I think that's what she meant. I also remembered while I hugged her, I kept apologizing because I assumed that it was my fault she was moving.

She kept telling me repeatedly:

"It's not your fault."

Eventually, I let go of her wondrous body and I left the classroom. But the drama didn't start until I got home. I got off of my bus, brought in the trash cans and saw my mom sitting on the porch. As I walked towards her, I suddenly started to shed tears of emotion. I was so overwhelmed with emotion from Mary moving that I just started to cry. I told my mom the entire story and I was crying as I told it. After I told her, I went to my room, got my *Verizon Touch Screen* phone, went to YouTube, and listened to *Why* and *Anything by 3T*. I even started to cry as I listened to the songs because they related to my situation so perfectly. I felt so broken inside. I didn't think I was never going to find another girl like Mary. I felt devastated. I felt alone. All I wanted was Mary. I thought I was never going to see Mary again . . . ***until my mom found her on MySpace.***

Another thing that I remember from 8th grade was when everyone in the school received a heart-stopping message. A 7th grade boy that went to school at East Lawndale had died. The cause of death was a stroke due to the fact that he was overweight. When I heard that report, all I felt was bad. I couldn't even think straight for one second. I even developed a feeling of paranoia and also a realization of the phrase "Life is short." I mean, if he died that quick, so can we. We can die at any time and not even know it. I mean, that one boy never got a chance to fully experience life and that's sad to me. Imagine . . . your entire life disappears in the blink of an eye. No one wants that. Especially not at an early age.

I felt sorry not only for the boy, but for the people that was so close to him. That boy may have been the most important person in another person's life and he's gone. He didn't even give a chance to fully experience life. That's a shame. I remember going home and being so paranoid that I thought that I was going to be next. That's when I went upstairs to my mother and asked her if she could run a blood test on me.

You see, my mother, way back when, taught nursing. She still had her own nursing gear, so she knew what to do. She had me jog in one spot as she timed me on her wristwatch. She tested my blood pressure and she had me breathe in and out as she listened to my heart with her stethoscope. I thanked my mother for carrying out the procedure and relieving me of my paranoia. But still, I was thinking about the boy and the life that he never got a chance to experience. That's why every day I try to leave a mark in remembrance of Jaylon Vishawn O'Neal because you never know what could happen.

Another thing that I remember was when I was in the East Lawndale yearbook for most school spirited. I remember how that all started. I was at a school pep rally and a teacher had the spirit stick in his hands. He came towards me with the stick and he gave it to me. I got up and showed people the reason I am who I am. I started dancing for everybody and everyone was in to it.

A couple of days after the rally, we were voting for people who were going to go in the yearbook for a specific category. Then, my name was underneath the category for "Most School Spirited" making it the 1st time I was nominated for anything in school. I mean, at first I was kind of surprised, but we all knew something like that was bound to happen sooner or later. The next day, the yearbook committee needed to take a picture of me and my girl friend named Leslie, who also won "Most School Spirited." It was awesome that they were taking my picture for the yearbook because that meant that I left my mark at East Lawndale. I left a mark for the future students of East Lawndale and I made it known who I was to the school. I was . . . *a boss!*

I remember trying out for my school basketball team. It was me, Corey and a whole bunch of other dudes that I knew that went to try-out. I was thinking about how the minute I got the ball, I was going to be "Like Mike."

I thought that I was suddenly going to get these unbelievable basketball skills the minute that I got the ball, but unfortunately it didn't happen like that.

For one thing, I didn't even have my gym clothes. I didn't know that I had to have them with me. I thought that I was done. I thought "Now I'll never get to play basketball." That's when this boy was gracious enough to lend me a pair of his shirt and shorts, so I could play. Aw, man! You do not know how grateful I was for that boy to lend me his shirt and shorts! Aw, man! I was so happy!

When we came out of the locker room to go to the court, we had to wait until the coach got there. It took nearly 1-2 hours just for him to get here and when he did, *man did we get worked!* The first thing we did was run around the basketball court for 8 minutes. The thing about me is I like to run, so when the bell rang, I ran full speed. Then, when 20 minutes passed, **I was out!** For the rest of the workout, I was trying so hard not to pass out! I was trying to work myself back up until the 8 minutes ran out and I succeeded without passing out! My lungs felt like they were bar-be-cued after we were done.

The 2nd thing that we did was the 3-point shootout practice where we started shooting 3-pointers all around the goal. I made 2/5 shots in that one drill! The 3rd thing that we had to do was shoot a lay-up and get pass the coach's defense. I planned in my head how I was going to execute my move and it was time to go, I went for it. But the problem was; I messed up. I couldn't get pass the coach and when I tried to shoot, he slapped the ball straight out of my hands. I waited on the side of the gym floor like everyone else until everyone finished their turn.

The last thing that we did was play scrimmage. When I played scrimmage with everyone, I didn't do too well. The minute I got the ball, a boy that was smaller than me took it away from me. Another thing that happened was when I was open and wanted the ball, no one would pass it to me. It was as if I was invisible and no one could see me. I felt as though I was given an unfair advantage the entire game, but I still kept at it. I would try to steal, block or take the ball away from someone, but no dice. I tried to at least get the ball to touch my fingertips, but even that was unsuccessful.

When the game was over, the coach created his roster of the people he wanted to represent the East Lawndale Boys' Basketball Team. When I went to look at the roster, my name wasn't on it. I got cut! Then I saw my dad walk over to the coach and had a little chat about me being cut. That's when the coach gave me the opportunity of being the manager of the Boys' Basketball Team. He started telling me how being the manager was the most important position in the game of basketball. I started thinking about all the things I could do if I was the manager. I thought it was going to be the bomb . . . *until I actually did the job.*

59

I would do a whole bunch of stuff for the team that I normally do at home. I picked up their jerseys and the shorts, washed them and gave them water when they needed it. I felt like I was the team's maid. It was if I was doing things for a bunch of disabled paraplegics! A couple of good things came out of being manager of the ELMS basketball team.

I got to practice with the team whenever I wanted and I got to go on every single last game that they played. Then, there was that one day where I finally got my chance to play with the team in a basketball team. I remember the day as if it was yesterday. I came in the gym at 10:00 A.M. just like I was supposed to only everyone else wasn't here yet. When everyone finally came, I put on my uniform and one of my teammates said:

"Now, you're one of us!"

After hearing that, I thought:

"Wow, I guess complaining and begging for a long time pays off!"

It wasn't until 2 hours later that people started to actually come inside the building for the game. Until then, we all chilled on the bleachers and waited for everyone to come and when people finally came, the coach wanted to dedicate the game to a young woman who died at the age of 22. After that, we started to play. We got on the court and did a few lay-ups just to prep for the game. I made 2 lay-ups and missed one that went off to the side of the rim. The horn rang and the team started to play, but I had to sit out. I was trying to figure out why I had to sit out when I could be playing with everyone else. It just didn't seem fair to me so I asked the coach:

"When am I going to play, coach?"

He said:

"Soon, Jaylon, soon."

To be honest, I was getting real impatient. That's when I started thinking. If everyone else is playing now, then I'll be later when the team gets enough points on the board. That made perfect sense! So I'm sitting on the bench waiting. Waiting for my chance to get on the floor. Waiting for my moment to shine. Waiting for my chance to show these people what I can do.

The 4th period finally came and that's when the coach put me in the game! He wanted me to do a play with the team that I didn't know anything about. I was confused on what to do, so I just started walking around the court until one of my teammates told me to stand in a certain position in front of them. I stood in the top left position of the court with my teammates and the game started. One of my opponents started dribbling the ball down the court trying to take it to the hole and I ended up losing the ball due to my "butterfingers." Then I noticed something. Every time one of my teammates got the ball, they would always pass it to me. I tried to shoot it, but it hit the rim and flew in the air. That's when my teammate jumped up, got the ball and scored. That was my 1st assist in any organized basketball game. One of my teammates dribbled the ball down the court when one of my opponents stole the ball away from him and that's when I stole it back! I dribbled down the court, but the ref blew the whistle because I "doubled".

That's when the coach did something that I never expected him to do. There were 30 seconds left in the game and he got everyone that was on the bleachers to cheer for me. Everyone was chanting:

"Jaylon! Jaylon! Jaylon! Jaylon"

I couldn't believe it! A crowd cheering my name in excitement. It was the most heartfelt cheer that I've ever heard in my life. I never expected anything like this! That's when I felt extremely warm all over my body! It was so unbelievably amazing! After 30 seconds, the horn sounded and I immediately ran to the coach, jumped up and gave him the biggest hug that I could possibly give. That's when I realized that just because you're not playing *with* the team does not mean you're not *on* the team.

"Talent without dedication is a daydream. Dedication without talent is a nightmare!"

-Mike Ditka

"Every great structure always needs a strong foundation."

-Coach

"If winning isn't everything, why do they keep score?"

-Society

Know who your real friends are
Make the woman you want the most important person in your life
Be your own team leader

Chapter 8

⚬◦❀◦⚬

9th grade. My experience in the 9th grade was so astounding, so exhilarating, and so crucial that it all has to be expressed in one phrase:

"It's a whole 'nother ball game!"

I started my high school career attending Bundy High. It was a school that was partnered up with a university in Georgia called Jefferson University. The partnership between the 2 schools gave students the opportunity to take free college classes at Jefferson University in their junior year of high school. At first, it sounded too good to be true to me until I went there and realized that it was a long way to go until we all went to that university. The biggest thing that everyone had to do to gain admission into JU is pass a test called the CRAFT test. The CRAFT test is normally a test that was only permitted for college students, but when Bundy High was formed, they made an exception.

When I was at Bundy High, the school lacked a few necessities.

One

We didn't have our own building and we were housed with another high school named Budrick High.

Two

We only had 3 classrooms that were in Budrick's building and all of our classrooms were in portables. So if it ever rained, we were screwed.

63

Three

We didn't have our own sports team, so if we wanted to play sports, we'd have to play for Budrick.

Four

The school board doesn't even realize Bundy High is a school.

Five

Not only was Bundy High housed with Budrick, but there was an annex for another school called Norwood.

With that being said, I'd like to talk about my experience there. When I was at Bundy High, I remember feeling happy yet paranoid. I was happy because I wanted to start the year off fresh and meet tons of new people! I was also paranoid because I had a feeling that I was going to be attacked by a group of people for absolutely no reason at all. But that was just me. Always ready to assume the worst out of something that I haven't even experienced yet. I mean, I let the stereotypical ways of modern media teach me everything that I needed to know about high school which is the wrong way to be taught about anything. I mean, I do remember that I was exposed to people smoking, seeing a condom wrapper on the bathroom floor, and a whole lot of fighting! I feel that the fights in the school increased my paranoia because you never know when and where one is going to start. But let's get back to my school, shall we?

The one thing that I remember was meeting Mr. Goons. Mr. Goons was one of the new teachers that started teaching at Bundy High on the same year I attended Bundy High. Mr. Goons was the type of person that liked to get along with everyone; he was a lot of fun to be around and was *real* patient with everyone. He didn't scream, yell, curse, or even talk slick at intolerant people. He may have gotten annoyed at people that didn't want to cooperate with him, but he did not show any sign of disrespect to anyone. At least, that was my opinion.

He was my homeroom teacher. I remember every time I would come into his classroom, I would always ask for a toothpick from him and that would be something that I would do every time I'm around Mr. Goons. I also remember how Mr. Goons and I would always have our famous chats in his class. We'd have our 15-minute chats about anything. We'd talk about the book *Mein Kampf* and what the title of the book meant. We'd talk about *The Godfather, Married With Children,* whatever we wanted to talk about. It was more like whatever *I* wanted to talk about.

Another thing that I remember from Mr. Goons was the time when the school was having individual Christmas parties in their classrooms. What Mr. Goons did for his party was bring in the **mother of all cases** . . . a silver case filled with his entire video game collection! He even had games from the PS2 in that chest! I almost cried when I saw all of those games in that one case! He said we were having a *Tekken* competition on his PS3 and I couldn't participate in it because I didn't have his class! I was a little upset that I didn't get to play in the tournament, but the fact that he was a die-hard gamer made all the difference that day!

Another thing that I remember about Mr. Goons was he always showed little or no emotion. It's like every time Mr. Goons would talk to people, he would always give them a blank expression. It was rare for him to smile at people. I remember him saying that it's because he has "100% control over his emotions." That's something that I wasn't able to do. I'm very emotional and that's been a problem for me ever since I was a child. I would always have no self-control over the way I would act.

I would always be the one to act silly around other people or say off-the-wall comments that would make people walk away. There were only a handful that stayed and they usually end up being my friends. It's something that I've been trying to readjust for a long time and I'm still struggling with it to this day. Mr. Goons has that one ability that makes everything in his life run smoothly which is something that I wish I could have. I mean, I had people reject me, yell at me, scream at me, use profane language towards me in a disrespectful manner and threaten me all because of the way I would act. It's gotten to the point where people can't even be in the same room as me without assuming that the next words that come out of my mouth will have them slamming their head into a door repeatedly until they become unconscious. I wished that instead of belittling me that they would've told me what I was doing wrong.

Another thing that I remember was meeting 3 people that would be the 3 main people that I would hang out with every single day at Bundy High. The first out of the three friends that I met was Daniel Roberts.

Daniel was the type of person that had a normal personality. He didn't try to get in trouble with anyone, he didn't try to be the center of attention and he didn't try to be upsetting to other people. He was always talking about the latest fashion or always trying to increase his "swag game".

Every day he would come to school wearing the hottest and latest fashion. He would always wear an Aeropostale shirt and if not an Aeropostale shirt, a Hollister shirt. If not a Hollister shirt, then an Adidas shirt. If not an Adidas shirt, a Nike shirt. If not a Nike shirt, a brand new pair of Adidas. If not Adidas, then Nikes. If not Nikes, then Levi's. If not Levi's, then Converse. And his shoes couldn't be old; they had to be fresh-out-the-box new! I mean, he cared *that* much about his appearance more than anything else in the world.

When it came to Daniel and me, we were always on a dead end street that just went nowhere! He cared about "swag", I could care less about "swag", how it's a word and why that's the main focus of my generation. I don't know, but these kids will die over "swag".

He talked about the NBA, I didn't. I mean, I love basketball with a passion, but talking about the statistics of other players, the teams that they would play for ***all day every day*** . . . nah!

He would talk about celebrity propaganda or the bull crap that plays on the radio every day; I could care less and would take my brain out of my skull before I get hooked to the garbage known as new school rap! ***I hate new school rap with an absolute and utmost passion!***

Another thing about Daniel was that he always loved trying to get under your skin. What I mean by that is he always loved reliving the past and trying to make a fool out of me. Everywhere I went; Daniel was always saying whatever he wanted to say about me to other people every day. I mean, at first we were joking around, but he doesn't understand the phrase "There's a limit to everything." That's how Daniel can come off as an annoying person especially towards me. With friends like that, who needs enemies?

Another friend that I had was named Ben Matthews. I've known Ben since I was in the 7th grade and I was surprised to see him attending the same school as me. Ben was the type of person that was quiet, patient, easygoing and didn't want a lot of attention. He wasn't exactly what I call "different" because, to me, he was an ordinary guy that didn't do anything abnormal. I mean, the only thing abnormal about Ben is that he wore caps everywhere he went. That's pretty much why I liked hanging out with Ben at times because he doesn't give anybody a hard time. That's why he's . . . cool.

The last friend out of the 3 friends benefited my life greatly. He not only showed me that you can do whatever you wanted to do regardless of how you look, but that you can always have fun by being yourself. Without him, I don't believe that I would have a strong character like I do now and I don't believe that I would be the lyrical emcee that I am now.

His name is Tiberius Godford. Tiberius had to be one of the smartest people that I knew. He knew a lot of things about the world that I didn't even know. He was also one of the funniest people that I knew. I mean, every word that came out of his mouth that revolved around a certain topic was always so funny that I would sometimes fall out of my chair! Tiberius also had a joke for everything no matter what it was and if someone made fun of his weight, then he would dog you out from head to toe until you wish that you didn't have a mouth!

Another thing about him was just like Daniel, he would talk about the latest fashion, wear Aeropostale, Hollister or Aerobrand and his favorite rapper was Lil Wayne. He absolutely _**loved**_ Lil Wayne! He knew about his life, his background and he loved all of his music! I mean, he cares about Lil Wayne just like I care about Michael Jackson. I also remember that he likes Kevin Hart. He knew his life, his family and loved all of his comedy shows! Every time that the 4 of us would have a conversation that involved comedy in any way, shape or form, he'd somehow manage to bring Kevin Hart into the mix. If not, he would quote a line that Kevin Hart would say from his comedy shows. Tiberius always managed to make every day fun and he didn't have to try so hard to do it. He was just being himself whether anyone liked it or not.

Put all of these 3 people together and you have my 3 friends that I spent 9th grade year with. Now we had some good times with each other, but the one time that I'll never forget was when Tiberius inspired me to rap.

We were all in Mr. Goons' homeroom roasting on each other like we do in every class that we had together. It wasn't until I shut Daniel up with whatever I said, but when it came to Tiberius, I was lost in words. I couldn't think of a clever comeback against him, so it was his turn. That's when he said, in the same rhythm as *The Jefferson's* theme song:

"Movin' on up
Longer pants
You need to pay your water bill
In advance!"

That's when it all clicked! Tiberius was the 1st person that I knew that could rap and made it sound good. It was like magic the way he said that rap which was something that I wanted to do too. After school, I got a pencil and a sheet of paper and wrote my first rap. I remember it was the corniest rap that I've ever written. I think it started off like:

"Hi, my name is Jaylon.
And I'm not playin'
I'm 'bout to show you

68

What I'm capable of doing
And that's pursuing
A rap career
You know the little thing
That makes you want to weep a tear
Yo, I'm the king
I do not sing
Doesn't anybody have a chicken wing?
Now let me tell you a little story
About the recent time of my former glory"

After that, I didn't know what the story was, but it was a start, right? Now when I went back to school the next day to show it off, a lot of people laughed and thought it was the funniest thing that they've ever heard. I even read it to these two girls and they laughed. I thought it was good until I got to the "chicken wing" part. That's when rapping was a regular thing that the group start to do now. When we were roasting, it was in lyrical form and when we weren't roasting, we were free-styling. At first, I started messing up by not saying the lyrics of my raps completely or I couldn't get the words out like I wanted to. That's when I started to practice. I started writing raps at home, practiced rapping my written rhymes privately and my work in school even started to become rhymes. I even rapped in class one day just to shut another boy up! But there was that one time that I will never forget where my rhymes were just so dope that I ended up making 2 out of my 3 friends mad.

You see, the one thing that Tiberius, Daniel and I had in common was we had a crush on 3 girls that were sophomores. Tiberius had a crush on a girl named Keisha, Daniel had a crush on a girl named Passion and I had a crush on a girl named Gabrielle.

Gabrielle was a gorgeous caramel-skinned beauty that always brought me down to my knees every time I would see her! Oh, man! She'd make me feel so alive!

Anyway, my Language Arts teacher Mrs. Morris was hosting her very 1st poetry slam in her classroom. She assigned all of her students to write a poem about whatever they wanted and I chose to write a rap about the 3 of us being in love with the 3 girls. It was called "Sophomore Fever." The thing that made Tiberius and Daniel ticked off at me was that I used their actual names in my song. (I didn't know you shouldn't do that! Come on! It was my 1st time performing in front of an audience!) And I didn't know that I was actually calling my boys out or "throwing them under the bus" if you will. When I was finished, everybody clapped and cheered because it was that amazing! That's when Tiberius said to me:

"We're done!"

I felt hurt and stupid inside. I didn't realize what I did wrong until I went to Mrs. Morris and she told me that I never should've used their actual names in the song.

That's when I said:

"Oh, now you tell me!"

I couldn't believe it! I lost both of my friends all because of my lyrics! I just couldn't believe it! They both acted as if I wrote a diss towards them! It was just me telling a story! I didn't know what to do now! I mean, I was alone now! I didn't have anyone to chill with except Ben! In my mind, I thought "Man, do I know how to mess things up!" It wasn't until next Monday that I went up to them and apologized to both Daniel and Tiberius.

At first, they didn't even want me to talk to them, but then I told them that I didn't know that I couldn't use their names in my rap. Daniel forgave me, but Tiberius didn't until a few minutes later. He said that we weren't friends, but he was going to be cordial towards me. That only lasted for a couple of days and then we acted as if it never happened. I guess that's what happens when you let time heal the wound.

Another thing that I remember was when I first met a boy named Malik Chambers. Malik was a boy that came straight out of New York.

I met him in my Civics class and he honestly knew a lot about where he was from right off the bat. For example, he knew right off the bat that the Statue of Liberty was a gift from France. When I asked him about it, he said:

"In New York, that was some of the things that you had to know."

He told me that in New York, aside from the bright lights and famous monuments, the one thing that New York was known for was its different types of cuisine.

There was a different part of town for every type of food that was served. The way he was talking about New York, it seemed as if it was hard for him to leave and start over again in a place he knew nothing about. It must've been difficult for Malik to adjust. I mean, Malik was a New Yorker and the last thing he wanted was to start over.

Another thing that I learned about Malik was he was a **mad** Mortal Kombat fan. He knew everything there was to know about Mortal Kombat. He knew the stories from the majority of the games created, he knew about the backgrounds of the characters in the game and he also knew how the game started out. He knows pretty much everything about that one video game!

To me, it was amazing to talk to a friend about something that I could relate to and the best part about it was we not only liked the same thing, but we acted the same way! Malik was like the brother that I never had! He made me feel like it was okay to be yourself no matter what anyone thinks of you! Life's too short to care about negative thoughts from negative people! That's the one motive of destruction that I've been getting all my life and I wasn't going to let it continue. I appreciate Malik for being the one to show me that and for being my friend.

Another thing that I remember was meeting a teacher named Mrs. Carrie. Mrs. Carrie was a woman that taught Advanced Compositional Language Arts on my 1st year of 9th grade. She was the type of teacher that would give so much homework that she's the reason deforestation happens. I remember the first day I walked into her class and I had to turn in summer reading assignments that Mrs. Carrie assigned over the summer. Those summer reading assignments literally took *forever* to complete and they made me have second thoughts about being at that school. Then I realized that it wasn't the end . . . *it was the beginning.*

For example, she made us get a composition book and told us that we had to write 5 pages on the literature that we would read. It didn't even matter what it was. It could've been the nutritional facts on the back of a milk carton. It could've been a book. It could've been a magazine. It could've been a billboard that you'd see on the highway. It could've been anything as long as it was written down in that notebook. When it came to me, I didn't take that under consideration that much. I tend to write 2-3 pages, procrastinate, and hurry up and write the last 2 pages before she started grading!

The one thing that I remember was when I was looking for my notebook. I looked all over the classroom until I saw it sitting right on her desk and didn't even know she had it! That's when I went off in her classroom! I started running all over the classroom like a maniac, yelling "I told you" repeatedly, so she could get the message. After Mrs. Carrie calmed me down, she told me that I had to write 20 pages for the 5 pages that I didn't write in the past 4 weeks. Hearing this, I had an expression on my face that said "Are you serious?!!" To be honest, everyone that knew Mrs. Carrie had the exact same feelings for her as I did. **We *didn't like her!*** It was like she was preventing students in her classroom from having a life outside of school because of all the work she'd give us and she would sometimes use her authority that she'd have as a teacher to tease her students. That's something that I wasn't fond of. That's when something glorious happened!

Mrs. Carrie told us that the school was having its annual pep rally and the students had an opportunity to pie a teacher. When I heard that, my attention span spiked straight through the roof! She told us that all we had to do to participate is to write a paper on why we wanted to be the one to pie a teacher and put money in the jar of the teacher that we wanted to pie. That's when I started writing a paper on why I wanted to be the one to pie Mrs. Carrie. After I was done, she read it in front of the class and everyone cheered in agreement.

When we went to lunch, the jars that we needed to put money were there. A lot of kids were crowded around the jars and I noticed that Mrs. Carrie's jar had the most amount of money in it because like I said, *everyone doesn't like her!*

When it was time for the pep rally, every single last kid had one thing on their mind: "Who was going to pie Mrs. Carrie?" I mean, that was the highlight of the entire thing! At least, that was my opinion. We started off the rally by doing a competition on who can pop the most balloons by sitting on them. I went up along with 4 other kids from each grade to participate. When the event started, I ran all the way to the seat at top speed and popped every single balloon that I was supposed to pop until it was over. I don't think I won, but I could care less. The next thing we did was a tricycle race on who could race from one side of the stage to the other. I couldn't participate because I already participated in the 1st event. It wouldn't be fair. I don't remember who won, but I do remember it wasn't us.

The 3rd thing that we did was a competition to see which grade had the most school spirit. The seniors went 1st and some of them yelled, but not everyone made an effort. Then the juniors went next and most of them yelled, but not as loudly. The sophomores went next and they yelled their hearts out. That means that we needed to blow the roof off of the entire building if we wanted to win, but when it was our turn we didn't do so great. We yelled, but not everyone yelled. The winners ended up being the seniors which we all called "shenanigans" on because they were graduating that year. After that . . . *it was about to go down!* It's that time where Mrs. Carrie announced who would be the one to pie her. She said that the winner of the contest was . . . *Malik!*

When I heard that Malik won, I brought both of my arms out and said:

"What? That's bull crap!"

The only reason Malik won was because he wrote a speech that wasn't bashing Mrs. Carrie. He spoke how we all felt, what we went through when it came to being in her class, and it made everyone in the classroom feel. Then, he ended it on a happier note by saying:

"Mrs. Carrie and pie have one thing in common, they're both sweet."

That's when everyone went "Aw" to what Malik said and cheered for him. He went on stage with Mrs. Carrie, put the pie in his hand and slammed it at her face!

That's when I stood up and cheered with everyone else at a messy Mrs. Carrie. She left the stage smiling with her face and jacket covered in pie with everyone laughing and cheering behind her. That's the day when I got my revenge on Mrs. Carrie because I may not have been the one to pie her, but I glad that I was there to see her get her "just desserts."

In life, you will always have the one person that you do not want to work with. Just do whatever you have to do with that person and go your separate ways.
Good friends are the people that will forgive you no matter what you do.
Make your own experience in life. Don't make other people's experiences your experiences. See for yourself what something is supposed to be before you judge it.

Chapter 9

One of the greatest memories that I had was when I met my friend Travis. Travis was a boy that lived in my neighborhood and he was always pleasant to be around. I remember the 1st time that we met each other as if it was yesterday. It was a sunny day and I was in the bathroom about to take a shower when someone knocked on the door. My sister, Jasmine, went to the door and answered it. She yelled:

"Jaylon! Some boy's here to see you!"

I went to the door as quickly as I could and I met this strange boy. He had on a black jacket, brown shirt, and a backpack with a tube coming out of it. I said:

"Hey! What's up?"

He said:

"Nothin'. How about you?"

I said:

"I'm good. How'd you know where I live?

He said:

"I saw you get off of your bus and I watched you go home."

I said:

"Oh. Well, I've been trying to figure out where you lived so I could meet you. But you beat me to it!"

He said:

"Well, let me show you where I live.

We both went outside and stood in the middle of my yard. He showed me where his house was located only I didn't know where he was pointing so I was totally lost.

He said:

"Why don't you come over later?"

I said:

"Yeah. I'll see you later."

That's when we both shook hands and we walked away from each other. One day after school, I went down the hill trying to find Travis. I remember that I went to a house that I thought was Travis's, but I was dead wrong. I ended up going to the house that was **next door** to Travis's house. I went to Travis's house and knocked on the door. A woman answered and I asked her:

"Hello ma'am. Does a boy named Travis live here?"

She said:

"Yes, Travis lives here, but he's not home.

I asked her:

"Do you know where he is?"

She said:

"He's at his friend's house. I'll bring him home if you like."

I said:

"Okay."

She got her phone, called Travis's friend and told him to come home. It took 10 minutes for him to get home and he came down the hill with his brother arguing about something. I didn't know what, but I did notice that they didn't like each other. I mean, the way that they were going back and forth reminds me of the relationship that I have with my brother. Travis saw me and said:

"What's up?"

I said:

"Nothin'. I was trying to find you."

He said:

"Oh. Well, I'm about to go in my house. Do you want to come inside?"

I said:

"Yeah, sure."

All 3 of us walked into his house and when I walked in, they had _absolutely_ _**no furniture.**_ If someone wanted to sit somewhere, it would be on the floor. I walked in and I met one of his sisters. She was the oldest out of the 3 and her name was Gloria. Before I got a chance to meet anybody else, I suggested that we go to my house.

I wanted to show Travis my house and let him meet my family. I let him and his brother come into my house and meet my mom, my step dad, my brother and sister. Then, we went downstairs and I showed him my *Nintendo Wii*. I showed him how it accessed special channels because it was connected to the Internet and we watched Internet videos on YouTube from my Wii.

I would show him clips from my favorite show *The Boondocks* and he would show me clips from his favorite TV shows. Another thing that I learned from Travis was that he was into anime. He loved *The Boondocks, Bleach, Naruto, Mega Man, Kingdom Hearts, Dragonball Z, etc.* He would literally talk about any anime that was on his mind and not get bored. He would go on and on about Dragonball Z and go on and on about Mega Man and go on and on about Naruto and so on and so forth. I mean, I love anime too, but he was a fanatic of the entire culture as a whole.

One thing that I remember about Travis was that in the beginning, he used to come to my house as early as 10 or 11 a.m. in the morning ready to hang out with me which became a problem *real* quick! That's when I had a little chat with Travis about <u>*boundaries.*</u> After that talk, he started coming to my house no later than noon or 1 p.m. wanting to hang out with me which was so much better. He would either want me to come to his house to play games or we would have one of our famous chats.

The one thing about our famous chats was we were free to speak our thoughts and feelings as openly as we wished. We would talk about anything in our chats. Video games, anime, the Boondocks, and we even talked about us. For example, he told me about his family and how he has a brother named D.J. who's on the "unrestricted side of life" meaning he does whatever he wants, watches whatever he wants to watch, says whatever he wants to say, leaves the house and comes back anytime he wants.

He also told me about his 3 sisters and how they each have bad habits. His oldest sister, Gloria, had a boyfriend that got her pregnant and now Travis was going to be an uncle.

His other sister, Tia, is a diva. She likes to flirt and she ran away more than once.

Then there's his last sister, Ciara, who's a smoker. She's been smoking since age 12 and she is 14 now. It's because of that nasty habit that got her kicked out of school.

As for Travis, he's pretty much the only sane one there. He goes to school, comes home every day to the same thing every day and he does it all while having scoliosis which is the reason why he's wearing his backpack with the tube coming out of it. (I think.) But we never talked about that.

Another thing that I remember about Travis was we had a lot of memories with each other and how they made us more knowledgeable about our environment. I remember one time Travis invited me to his house to meet his cousins only things didn't go quite as I hoped it would. Travis and I were playing video games on his Wii when all of a sudden; one of his cousins came through the door and shot me in my leg! That's when I said:

"Ow! What the heck is going on man?"

Travis said:

"I don't know, but are you O.K?"

I said:

"Yeah, I'm good! But what is going on?!

Just then, one of Travis's cousins came through the door and I immediately said:

"Don't shoot!"

He didn't shoot. Instead, he told us that we were involved in some kind of battle of the sexes.

79

Immediately, Travis and I said:

"Uh uh! No way! We don't want to be involved!"

Out of the blue, 3 girls came into the room and they started blasting their guns at us as if their guns were the real deal. I got shot in the leg *again,* shot in the chest and my other leg. Travis got shot in his chest and the other dude started shooting with his Nerf rifle at the girls. The girls left and that's when me and Travis got out of the room as quickly as possible, but when I did, D.J. stabbed my leg twice.

Again, I said:

"OW!"

Then I looked at D.J. and said:

"For real, man?! For real?!!

We fought our way through the barrage of bullets that came our way and we made it outside only to find Travis's cousins playing there too. Both of us ran all the way up the hill to my house, so we could come up with a plan. We sat on my steps talking about how hurt we were over our wounds that we got from the Nerf bullets and we questioned the fact that Travis's cousins would engage in that type of activity. That's when I got an idea! We fight back! We go down there, get a Nerf gun and fight back!

When we got down there, no one was shooting their bullets! That's when Travis and I got a gun, went into a room with a wall full of Nerf bullets, loaded our guns with them and we waited. I sat down on a sofa waiting anxiously for someone to shoot me. Travis's mom sat down next to me and saw me with a Nerf gun that was full of bullets. At that exact moment, she put a stop to it! She made everyone in the house aware of what was going on based on my description on how everything went down! That's when everyone gave their guns up, Travis's cousins got in trouble and Travis and I went back to playing video games.

Travis said:

"Man, am I glad that's over!

I said:

"So am I dude! So am I!"

Travis's mom came through the door and asked us if we wanted something to eat. Realizing that we were so hungry, we got up, went to the kitchen, loaded our plate with whatever we wanted to eat and had the dinner of champions!

Another thing that I remember was when Travis and I did community service. I had to do community service for school and I didn't feel like doing it by myself, so I got Travis to help me out. We went around the neighborhood collecting cans, beer bottles, chip bags, soda bottles, anything we could find and put in our trash bags. As we were walking around the neighborhood, an old man in a red convertible immediately drove down the road, stopped right in front of us and asked us questions about the Bible. At first, I thought he was one of Travis's relatives, but then I realized that he wasn't.

The man asked us:

"Are you Luke, John, Peter, Matthew, Mark, Samuel?"

We both looked at him and said:

"No!"

He asked us:

"Do you look like your father?"

We both looked at him nervously and said:

"No!"

The old man asked us:

"Do you have blond hair?"

We both said:

"No!"

The old man asked us:

"Do you believe that Jesus Christ is the son of God?"

We both said:

"Yes!"

We stood there for a good 2 minutes trying to figure out why this man was asking us all of these bizarre questions about the Bible and why we felt glued to the pavement. I mean, as much as I wanted to run away, I couldn't because I had a fear that he would chase us in his car and run us over.

After he was done, he drove away at top speed in his car and all me and Travis did was laugh. I mean, it was a funny experience that we never expected to see and it also brought life to the age old phrase "Expect the unexpected." A nearby woman saw us and she asked us:

"Did you boys know that man?"

We both said, happily:

"No!"

We walked down the road until we sat down at a park bench to rest. We laughed until our lungs froze from the cold or until Jesus came for the 3rd coming. Either way, it would be a long time before we stopped laughing. But out of all things, I'm glad that I spent a day with a good friend. A good friend that's always there when I need him, a good friend that understands my weirdness and a good friend that understands me as a person. That's why Travis is the guaranteed definition of what a true friend is.

Another thing that I remember was when this stray and feral dog was terrorizing my block. He was a purple dog that had the similar characteristics of *Cujo*. He was mean, vicious and had an intent to kill if he saw you. I mean, this dog was so mean that he made one of my neighbors from across the street jump on top of his car. I mean, if you wanted to go somewhere, you would have to look around to see if he was in the street or in your yard waiting on you. I remember a time where I had an encounter with the dog face-to-face. It all began when my mom was trying to get our ginormous television set placed in the living room.

My mom and I were the only 2 people in the house and my dad wanted to put his dad's T.V. in the den downstairs, so we had to put the ginormous T.V. upstairs. Both of us picked up the T.V. and carried it all the way up the concrete walkway until we reached the stairs. From that point, we both couldn't lift it up so I called Travis.

When he got the call that we needed help, he came to my house faster than *The Flash*. He saw that we needed help and he picked up the T.V. set. All 3 of us carried it into the house and placed it in the living room and just when we did, my step dad, siblings and a bottle of *Sprite* came home.

After that was said and done, I walked Travis back to his house and just as we were about to go down the hill, there he was. ***The dog.*** He barked ferociously at us repeatedly and that's when I told Travis to:

"Back away slowly."

As I slowly retreated, I was looking for an object of some sort to use against him in case he would attack us. The dog stopped barking and went back to wherever he was. Right at the moment, I told Travis the next thing we needed to do was:

"Run like heck!"

We ran all the way back to his house only to find his entire family sitting on their couch watching *Bebe's Kids*. We both fell on the couch, trying to catch our breath. Then, we both ran into a big problem: How was I supposed to get home? I had 2 options:

1   Walk up the hill and face the dog again.
2   Take the long way back.

I took the long way back home. I just couldn't face that dog again. It would be too risky. I started running the entire way home because I wanted to get home as quickly as possible. When I reached home, I went up the stairs to tell my mom about the encounter, but she wasn't paying attention. So I left the room and went to my room. At that moment, I started thinking about Travis and what he did. He helped this family with a difficult task even if he didn't want to. He was also there when I encountered the dog face-to-face. He was there for me when everyone else didn't want to be. Man, am I glad to have a friend like Travis in my life!

Another thing that I remember was when I took Travis with me to *The Hot Spot*. It was Saturday night and my mom wanted to know if I wanted to go. I said "Yes" without hesitation.

My mom also said:

"Why don't you see if Travis wants to go?"

I said:

"O.K., I'll go to his house and ask him."

That's when I hung up the phone, walked out the door and went straight to his house. At first when I asked him, he wasn't into the idea of going out until I had to constantly beg for him to come with me. After 5 minutes of begging, he finally accepted. He took a shower, put some clothes on and we left the house. I told Travis that he needed to contact his mom before we went anywhere and when that was said and done, we went to *The Hot Spot*.

When we got inside the skating section of The Hot Spot, there was a huge line that led all the way to the entrance of the skating rink which is where we were. It took us 3 minutes to get our wristbands and go inside to get skates. The bad part about it is the staff couldn't hold my shoes like they always do because apparently kids go behind the counter and steal other people's shoes. I mean, really?!! I couldn't even skate because I didn't know where to put my shoes and Travis wasn't having a good time either. All he did was stand in one place waiting to go back home. I tried to get him to mingle with other people, but he couldn't because he didn't know anybody. Well, this is great! My entire Saturday night . . . **ruined!** Could this night get any worse? That's when it did.

A fight broke out in the middle of the floor between 2 boys. Everyone in the arena was crowded around the 2 boys. That's when the police intervened and pulled the 2 boys away from each other. The staff even got to the point where every single person in the arena had to sit on the ice until everything got straightened out.

After 3 minutes, they let everyone skate again and I just decided to return my skates because what sense did it make to skate knowing that I can't put my shoes anywhere? I returned my skates, exited the arena and went upstairs to watch everyone skate from the top floor. Eventually, I got bored and went outside of the building and that's where things started to get worse. Everyone was outside either starting drama with the police, trying to get home or starting drama with other people. I mean, every second of the minute, people were fighting each other. They either wanted attention or they were very upset with another person over nothing. My mom finally drove up and saw the ruckus going on. She immediately gathered everyone into her car and we drove away.

As we were driving, we saw people from *The Hot Spot* walking down the street trying to get ran over. I was so mad at everything that happened that I started apologizing to Travis for dragging him into all of this. Even though it was unnecessary for me to apologize because I didn't cause the mayhem. I just wanted to spend some time with Travis because I remember 2 weeks ago; he said that he was moving away from my neighborhood. That would mean that if he left, then I would have no one to hang with. I would have no one to play chess with. I would have no one to play video games with. I would have no one to watch YouTube videos with. I would have no one in the neighborhood that actually understood me. I would have lost my one true friend. That's why before he moved, I told him that you are the one that can turn your family around. You are the one that can make a better future for yourself. You are the one that can make the world a better place. You are the one that can change how you live your life. And you are also the one that can make all of the difference in the world. After that, I never saw him again. Travis . . . the one friend that I'll always keep in my heart.

Always know who your true friends are because, these days, true friends are hard to come by.

Chapter 10

⟨❄⟩

Over the summer, the School Board voted unanimously to give Bundy High its own building, so it was "Goodbye Budrick". The building that the School Board gave us was formerly a teen pregnancy center called BAP. When I first seen the school, it matched Bundy High perfectly because just like Bundy High is lacking a few necessities, so was the building itself. It was the building that I was going to spend my 10th grade year at. Only this year, things played out a bit differently.

In the tenth grade, I started my school off in a brand-new building with brand new people. We all had to wait in the cafeteria until the bell rang so I decided to mingle with some old and new people. I went to say "Hello" to Tiberius, but he made it known that he didn't want to be bothered by me. The reason being is something that happened over the summer. You see, I was talking to Tiberius via Facebook messaging and I must've said something that made him annoyed with me. That's when I decided to let "Time heal the wound." As for Daniel, I didn't hang around him because he was going to be the same annoying dude that always tried so hard to get under my skin. I remember seeing new faces and familiar faces that I never expected to see.

One new person that I met was named Tyson. Tyson was a new boy that transferred from another school called Madison High School. At first, he was a person that didn't want to be bothered with a lot of people. I remember saying "Hello" to him on the 1st day and he didn't say "Hello" back until the 3rd time. I also remember one time; I pushed his button when I talked about the fact that he was homosexual to my friend Rodrigo. Another thing that I learned about Tyson was that he was extremely sensitive of his homosexuality. I mean, he doesn't care who knows he's gay but he gets highly offended when you tease him because he's gay. He also hates it when you call him a word that starts with an "f" and rhymes with "rabbit." He's offended by that word the same way black people are offended when they're being called the "n word" by a white person. I mean, I remember we were playing *Call of Duty: Black Ops* and some people in the lobby started calling him the "f" word. He felt so hurt that he left the lobby and didn't want to be bothered with anyone. I mean, he may be gay and act like a woman around people, but that's who he is. I mean, who are we to tell people who we can and can't love? Who he's attracted to is his business. That's all that matters. And the fact that he's gay never stopped him from being my friend.

Another familiar face that I seen again was a girl that I went to East Lawndale with. Her name was Cailee and she was a pretty nice girl. She was nice to talk to, beautiful, sophisticated, and bright. I was glad that I was going to have her as a classmate because she already knew who I was on the spot. I believed that we were going to have a good year together until one day I said one thing that made Cailee see the other side of me.

We were both in homeroom and it was the last 5 minutes of class. We were all in class reading the School District handbook. When we were done, it was free time. A minute later, Cailee and her friends were having a good enough day to want to sing "Celebrate". Then she said that one line that killed me!

She said:

"There's a party going on!"

After that, I said:

"Yeah, and it's in your pants!"

At that point, Cailee had me on lockdown and I didn't even know it because the next day, I was in trouble. My homeroom teacher, Mrs. Morris, called me back into her classroom when it was over and she told me that I was written up for my comment towards Cailee. Here's what I was thinking:

"Are you serious?!!"

I waited in my 2nd block class until my principal, Mrs. Farris, brought down the hammer on me. I mean, the entire time I was in there, that's all I was thinking about the entire time that I was in there. It wasn't until an hour later that she finally came in and brought me into her office. She said that the comment that I said was disgusting, uncalled for and could land me in jail for sexual harassment. The entire time I was sitting in there listening to her, my nervous system shot up through the roof! I felt like I was sitting in the electric chair! She told me that Cailee was upset at me for what I said and she could've pressed charges against me if she wanted to. That's when I sunk lower in my seat.

She said:

"Why could you say there's a party going on in your shoes? That's where your feet are! You got to watch what you say to people! You got to also think before you speak! Now, I'm going to call Cailee up here and you are going to apologize!"

She called Cailee to the office to tell her side of the story. When Cailee came in, she pretty much talked about everything that happened in the classroom, what type of action she took towards the incident and how it made her feel. Mrs. Farris explained to Cailee that my inappropriate comment was just me trying to be cool, not knowing how far off she was, but I just let her talk. Cailee also brought up a moment where we were sitting together on the bus and she talked about how I stared at her chest the entire time. Mrs. Farris's mouth dropped to the floor when she heard that. That's when I immediately jumped up and said:

"That is not true! I don't remember any of that happening!"

Then Mrs. Farris said:

"Now, do you realize what you just said? "That is not true" and "I don't remember" are two different phrases that have 2 different meanings. "That is not true" means that it never happened. "I don't remember" means that it can be proven to be true."

After that, she wanted me to apologize to Cailee and she wanted me to give a sincere and honest apology. At that point, I made the most honest and sincere apology that I could think of. I got in front of her, got down on one knee and said:

"Cailee, I apologize for my inappropriate comment towards you. What I said was stupid and dumb and I promise that I will never hurt you ever again. Do you accept my apology?

She looked at me once and said:

"Yes, I do."

After that, Mrs. Farris looked at me and told me:

"Jaylon, you can't go through life making comments like that to people. It's okay to joke around with people, but you also got to know when enough is enough. Do you understand me?"

I said:

"Yes ma'am."

She let both of us leave the office and then the bell rang. 3rd period began and I was on my way to class. As I walked down the hall, I started thinking about all the time in the past where I've gotten myself in trouble because of the unnecessary comments that came out of my month and thought:

"Dang! I really don't know when to stop!"

Something is wrong with me, but I promise you if it had been anybody else, Cailee wouldn't have said anything! But let's get off that topic for a minute! Let's talk about one good thing that came out of that school year! I remember that I had a great sweet 16th birthday. It may not have been on MTV or anything, but it was good enough for me! It all started when I was in school.

I came to the school wearing my *Cat in the Hat* chain trying to look my very best for my birthday. It was also the same day the school was having its first school dance at the new building. It was also the dance where I would be performing my rap that I wrote about how I first started out. (That is if Mrs. Farris remembers which I highly doubt). Later that day, I remember going home only to be welcomed by a message on a dry erase board written by my mother in red marker saying:

{Happy 16th B-Day, Jaylon!}

She was waiting for me to walk through the door so she could give me a big hug. When she was done hugging me, she told me to go to the table and there was a birthday cake made entirely out of vanilla and chocolate cupcakes waiting for me on the table. I took a chocolate cupcake and as I was eating it, she started singing "Happy Birthday" to me. After the wonderful serenade she said she needed to speak to me in private so we went upstairs to her room when I came into the room, she wanted me to close the door. My mom wanting me to close the door meant that it was going to be a something heavy. I sat on her bed and waited for her to speak.

She looked at me, concerningly and said:

"Jaylon, you are autistic."

I responded:

"Artistic? Mom, I already know that, it runs in the family."

She said:

"Boy, I'm being serious. You are autistic."

And I responded

"Explain."

And she did in depth. Finding out was great! I felt like I was introduced to the left side of my body. At that moment, everything made sense. I know the reason my mom kept it from me was because she didn't want me to "become autistic". She didn't want me to have a reason not to be successful. ***No excuses! Failure is not an option!*** I believe that everything comes to knowledge when it's supposed to.

After that, my little brother and sister ran in the room and gave me birthday cards. I remember the funniest one that I gotten was the one from my mother. It was a birthday that listed 10 things that she's glad that I don't do. I don't remember the entire list, but I do remember that 2 things from the list. She's glad that I'm not on the FBI's Most Wanted list and that I don't come home with loose women. That birthday card alone made my day! She also gave me $100 in spending money and I already knew where I was going to spend it! Straight to *GameStop*! We went into GameStop to get the brand new *Sony 7.1 Wireless Surround Sound Headset* that I saw in my latest issue of *GameInformer Magazine*. We went in, got the Headset and then she drove me to the dance. I went to the dance and saw a good 20-30 people in the building. I mean, every time the school has a dance, not that many people go because they would have dances on a Friday. That's a bad decision because everybody in Georgia knows that every Friday; everyone is at a basketball game. I went over to where my friends were and I started hanging out with them. I talked to Rodrigo about the dance and he said:

"I was going to be here until 8:30 and leave."

I said:

"Why do you want to leave so early?"

He said:

"I just wanted to see how this dance was going to go and leave."

I said:

"Oh, ok!"

I started walking around the dance floor, saying "Hello" to everyone that was there, drinking sodas and eating chips. You know, keeping it casual. One thing that I remember was that this girl Chloe was dancing with the rest of my friends and I decided to join them. I was behind Chloe when I trying to dance and the minute I shook something, it caused a problem. Chloe turned around and thought that I was trying to "get all up in the trunk" and went somewhere else. But I swear; I wasn't trying to put a move on her! My friends were talking about how they were going to have to tell Mrs. Farris even though I told them that I wasn't trying to put a move on her. Feeling upset at myself, I just sat down in a seat, took out my earphones, and listened to music.

A couple of minutes later, there's an announcement from the DJ who was a local radio personality.

He said:

"Yo, where my man, Jaylon, at?"

Everyone in the room looked right at me and I walked up to the stage. Everybody started clapping and cheering as I walked up the stairs. Confused, I asked:

"What's going on?"

I found out that Mrs. Farris put in a special request to get everyone in the room to recognize the fact that it was my birthday. That's when everyone in the room started singing "Happy Birthday" to me.

I couldn't believe it! It was just like 4th grade when everyone in the cafeteria sang "Happy Birthday" to me. I felt loved. I felt like people actually cared about my existence. I felt extraordinary in the eyes of my fellow students. I actually felt like the guest of honor. I mean, they could've done it just to get it over with, but hey . . . it's my day! And it was awesome!

Another memory that stuck out to me in tenth grade was when I got in trouble again for doing the exact same thing to another girl. Her name was Hailey and she was a brilliant, gorgeous and smart young girl that loved playing sports. She played volleyball and softball and her favorite person to fantasize over is Justin Bieber. She loved Justin Bieber **_with a passion that was unexplainable!_** She was practically obsessed with the guy! I mean, she's pretty much in the crowd of boy crazy girls that want to be Justin Bieber's everything and would be absolutely devastated if something tragic were to happen to him. But enough about that! Let's get back to the story.

One day, Rodrigo, Hailee, and the rest of my friends were coming back from lunch. We all walked down the hallway until we got to our math teacher's classroom. As usual, we had to wait until he opened his door. To pass the time, we all started being silly with each other and that's when me and Rodrigo started being silly towards Hailey. I remember that I was used to call Hailey "vanilla ice cream" because it was my cute nickname for her and she would laugh every time I'd call her that. I also started talking about how great Ebay is for some reason and Rodrigo said that:

"Ebay is awesome!"

I mean, I was talking so much about Ebay that I even did my own customized Ebay dance in front of Hailey. She laughed when I was doing the dance because it was me being silly as always. My math teacher, Mr. Naffas, finally came down the hall and he unlocked the door and we all went into his classroom. Pretty much a normal day, but with an abnormal twist!

The next day, I was called to the office because I was written up a 2nd time for sexual harassment and, get this, racism! (Racism?! Really?!) The dance that I did was counted as sexual harassment because of the way it was performed and the fact that I did it in front of a teenage girl. She also talked about how the "vanilla ice cream" part counted as racism. (Are you kidding me? It was just a pet name)!

She said to me:

"It says here in the School District handbook that in 1984 after they were trying to establish homosexual rights . . . that you can't discriminate anyone based on race, color, gender, ethnicity, sexual orientation or religion. You can go to jail for what you called Hailey."

I told her:

"Mrs. Farris, I wasn't trying to be racist towards Hailey. I was just trying to make a nickname for Hailey."

She asked:

"Ok, and why did you call her "vanilla ice cream"? Because she was white?"

I said:

"Yeah."

She said to me:

"But you can't say things like that! Imagine if Hailey were to run all the way home crying to her parents all because of what you said! Then, her parents would want to press charges!"

I said to Mrs. Farris:

"Well, she wasn't acting like that yesterday so why is she acting like this now?"

Mrs. Farris said:

"Because, that may have been how she acted, but that's not how she felt. You have to take other people's feelings into consideration. Understand how they feel before you start saying whatever you want."

I said:

"Yes ma'am."

She told me:

"That's 2 strikes!"

I asked her:

"What do you mean?"

She said:

"I'm going by the baseball method. The 1st strike was with Cailee and the 2nd one is with Hailey. 3 strikes and you're out of this school!"

I said:

"Yes ma'am."

I left the office and went back to class. I felt like my days at this school were numbered. I felt that everyone had the advantage over me. All they needed to do is make up a lie, get a whole bunch of people to believe in that lie and I'm screwed! I felt like I was at war between my haters and my friends and I kept losing people either because of insulting comments that comes out of my mouth or because of the way that I acted or because I did it. I couldn't do anything! The exact same comment from anyone else would've been a word of passion, but coming from my mouth made it racist and sexual harassment! But why? I didn't mean any harm, but I'm treated as a common crook. Take Malik for example.

Remember in ninth grade how we were the best of friends and we liked each other's company and all that good stuff? Well . . . in 10th grade, everything fell apart. You see, every time I was hanging out with Malik, he was always ignoring me. He acted as if I was invisible every time I was near him. I mean, he'd say "Hello" to me and everything, but when it came to other people, it was instant avoidance. Either that or my craziness shut everything down. I even got to the point where I had to imitate him just to get him to want to be around me. I remember one event that reminded me of the fun me and Malik had and also how he stopped being my friend.

There was an annual convention at JU called Nerd-a-thon and I was so psyched about going! There was going to be people dressed up like their favorite characters from their favorite animes, portraits of anime characters, toys, comic books, 12-sided dice, that sort of thing, but I wasn't going for that. I was going because they had a video game section of the convention where you can play brand new video games and old classics for free. So I get there and I started watching people play *Rock Band*. I also saw *Modern Warfare 3* which, at the time, was the game that I was absolutely willing to kill someone over so I went over and watched people play the game. Me and Rodrigo have been talking about *MW3* every day that year because, to us, it was the one of the most anticipated games of that year! At Nerd-a-thon, they had all kinds of games on different types of platforms like Zelda would be on the Wii; Mortal Kombat would be played on the 360 and Batman: Arkham City would be on the PS3.

As I watched people play the games, I also saw Malik by the entrance of the video game section. I went over to where Malik was at and said:

"Hey, Malik!"

He looked and saw me coming towards him and he shook my hand.

I asked him, in excitement:

"What are you doing here?"

He said:

"I'm here with Sam."

Sam was a girl that was like Malik's sister because they always liked hanging out with each other. Almost as if they formed a lifelong bond.

I said:

"Oh, ok!"

I started hanging with Malik and Sam until we met up with these 3 girls that go to our school. That's when Malik started chasing the girls around the building. I followed to see where it was going. After that, we started chilling outside. Me and Malik wanted to do something crazy so we both jumped on top of a roof. Then we saw campus police in the midst, so we got off the roof as quick as we could. After that, Malik rolled down the grass with Sam or one of us pushed down a low hill and he got grass all over his jacket.

Malik said, happy yet bummed said:

"Oh man! Now I have to get my jacket washed and . . ."

Then I added:

" . . . degrassed."

He said:

"Degrassed."

As he was getting grass off of his coat, I asked him:

"Hey, Malik. How do you have so many friends?"

He said:

"Just be yourself."

And that's exactly what I did. Throughout the entire day I was at Nerd-a-thon, that's all I did. I listened to music with Malik. I beat Malik and Sam in a foot race. I played Rock Band with other people while Malik watched. I watched Malik get his butt whipped about Mortal Kombat. (He was playing it on the 360 even though he's used to playing it on the 360). I played Truth or Dare with Malik, Sam and the 3 girls. Then I had to leave, but all in all, it sounded like a nice night out, right? But then one day, he did this.

We had an all-boys conference at school to get us prepared for the CRAFT test and college life at JU and I was just being myself by asking beneficial yet unnecessary questions. But it wasn't what happened during the conference, it was what happened ___after___ the conference. We met up with our friend Rosie and Malik told Rosie about how I acted during the conference. He also brought Nerd-a-thon and he said:

"You kind of embarrassed me when we were at Nerd-a-thon! I mean, he was chasing all of the girls all over the Chester Center!"

When I heard that, I thought:

"How do you call someone an embarrassment, but you act the exact same way? And that was *you that* chased the 3 girls around the building! Not me, *you*! But you're so quick to tell what I did, but not what you did! Okay! I got'cha!"

At that point, I just didn't want anything to do with Malik. I mean, I just couldn't deal with him ignoring me, talking about me behind my back and always choosing to get irritated at me every time I would comment on his Facebook posts. I had enough! So I just stopped talking to Malik and eventually, he got the message. Another one bites the dust!

Another thing that I remember was when someone wrote a disrespectful message about me on the bathroom wall. I was in the bathroom one day taking care of "business" when I saw a message written in blue permanent marker saying:

{*Jaylon likes men*}

When I saw that, I didn't scream or cry or get mad at myself. I simply laughed because people at this school actually think that something as little as a message on the bathroom wall is going to bring me down! I mean, I felt bad a little because people chose me as a target and it was also proof that I have haters at my school. When school was over, I went home and told my mom the whole story. Surprised at what she had heard, she told me to get someone to take a picture of it and show it to Mrs. Farris. And that's exactly what I did. I got Mr. Goons to come with me to the bathroom and see the message. He brought out his IPhone, took a picture of it and got rid of the message using his magic eraser which looked like a big, white sponge. He also started taking pictures of other things that was on the wall like stupid drawings, idiotic messages, etc. From then on, nobody wrote on the bathroom walls ever again. (Well, at least not yet).

Two Months Later

---•❋•---

Two months had passed and it was finally time for me to take the dreaded CRAFT test (college admissions test) at JSU. I never thought that getting into college would be so hard, but then again, I was wrong. I was terrified. The room was filled with college hopefuls who would, one day, roam the halls of Jefferson University. It was time to take the test and, to be honest; I thought I had it in the bag. I was so sure that I nailed it. I was so sure that I began picturing myself in a Jefferson University T-shirt.

I also started having visions of being in a college classroom with my other classmates learning from the brilliant mind of my college professor and meeting a lot of college girls that would take a fine interest in my intellect or meet a whole lot of people around campus that were happy to see me. I was so confident that I was going to pass this test . . . ***until I got back my results***.

I aced one part of the test, but not the other. Are you serious?! It was true! I failed by one point and I would have to wait until next year to try again. When I found out that I wasn't going to Jefferson University, I didn't even want to go to school anymore. I just wanted to run away. I was extremely upset that I wanted to take my anger out on the university itself because I felt that there was a conspiracy in the university. It was as if the staff of Jefferson University didn't want me there. That's when I talked it over with my mom and we went over the questions that I could remember and, after talking with her, I realized that "to infer" in a story setting was not familiar to me. I didn't quite get it until now. That's why I love my mom because she can make things easier for me to understand. Like I said she's my rock, sword and shield. In the end, I guess it wasn't my time, but next year that's a different story. Jefferson University, I'll see you soon because *I won't stop! I won't quit! And I will never give up!*

My day to day life is hard, but I wouldn't trade it for all the riches in the world. I am impulsive at times, but over the years I've learned how to control that behavior. I try to listen before I speak, I don't repeat myself as much, I pick up on social cues that once had me clueless and I give people their personal space. I also had to forgive all the people in my life who judged me and asked for patience from the people that I've wronged in word, thought or deed.

Life is funny because people try so hard to be different and they choose to ridicule the one thing that they desire to be.

That's why I love being different because no matter what, *I'm always going to be different! You might choose me as a target and try to bully me but I'm fighting back! You may leave me out and not invite me to parties but I'm crashing! You may even count me out or hate on my dreams but I'm winning, I'm surviving, I'm still here believing in my dreams and with faith, the reward is on the way so don't wait on me to fail because my success is meant to be and ordained just for me and I won't stop until its complete. After all, the hardest struggles are given to the strongest warriors.*

Epilogue

•❖•

I want to be in the lives of people that have trouble coping with autism. I want to show children, teens, and adults that having autism is absolutely nothing to be ashamed of. It doesn't mean you're dumb. It doesn't mean you're slow. It doesn't mean you're stupid. It doesn't mean you're insane. It doesn't mean you're weak. It means you're human and we are all different. Everybody's different in their own unique way. And that's what autism is. Pure uniquity. People with autism live happy lives every day and they are one of the smartest people on this earth. They can be doctors, lawyers, businessmen, politicians, judges, actors, athletes, authors, CEOs, celebrities, etc. You could have autism. Autism doesn't discriminate. But it's up to you to either make it a crutch or make a difference with it. This book is dedicated to the millions of people around the world without a voice. Without a person in the world to call a friend, without a person in the world that's willing to help them in their time of need, without a person that will listen to what they have to say, without a person that will understand their thoughts and feelings. This book is dedicated to the people that have been hated, neglected, abused, and tormented around the world every day. This book is dedicated to the people whose cries for help go unanswered. This book is dedicated to all the people who feel that they have nowhere else to turn. This book is dedicated to the people who have been deemed wrong by the judgmental society in which we live.

Jaylon V. O'Neal

Reflections

To all the people who read this book, I leave you with this.

Always love yourself no matter what. Treat every day as if it was your last. Live life to its fullest and never be afraid to express yourself! Always be yourself no matter what happens because it's not about other people's opinions, it's about yours. Always feel free in your own skin. Do what you feel is right. Make your own choices. Leave your own mark. Be strong and be your own leader. Yes, this world can be a scary place, but it's up to you to stand up and fight back. Also, know that we may be of different colors, different backgrounds, different religions, different ethnicities, different cultures, but there is only one race and that's the HUMAN RACE! WE ARE ONE!

Unity for you and me
Hand and hand, together we stand
We should always love and respect one another
We are all sisters and we are all brothers
Fight for me and I'll fight for you
Hear my words because they're true
You are strong and mighty, not feeble and weak
I AM AUTISM, HEAR ME SPEAK!

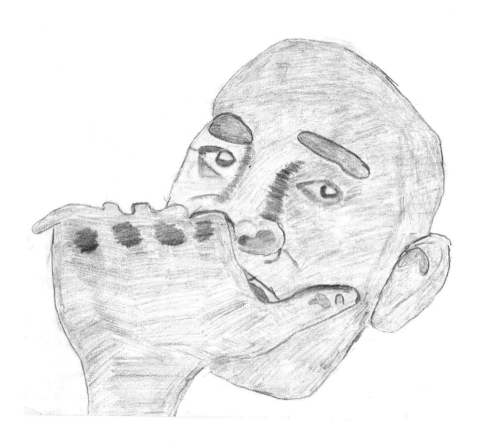

Sketched by Jaylon O'Neal